P. Vanderbur

On Reflection

AN AUTOBIOGRAPHY

ON REFL

WITH SANDFORD DODY

HELEN HAYES

ECTION

AN AUTOBIOGRAPHY

Published by M. Evans and Company, Inc., *New York*
and distributed in association with
J. B. Lippincott Company, *Philadelphia and New York*

To Charlie and Mary
PAST AND FUTURE

My dear Grandchildren,

At this writing, it is no longer fashionable to have Faith; but your grandmother has never been famous for her chic, so she isn't bothered by the intellectual hemlines. I have always been concerned with the whole, not the fragments; the positive, not the negative; the words, not the spaces between them. I loved and married my Charlie, your grandfather, because he was both poem and poet. What wonders he could work with words.

From your parents you learn love and laughter and how to put one foot before another. But when books are opened you discover that you have wings.

No one can tell me that man's presence on earth isn't expected—even announced. Because the magi come to each new babe and offer up such treasures as to dazzle the imagination. For what are jewels and spices and caskets of

7

gold when compared with the minds and hearts of great men?

What can a grandmother offer in the midst of such plenty? I wondered. With the feast of millenia set before you, the saga of all mankind on your bookshelf, what could I give you—Jim's children? And then I knew. Of course. My own small footnote. The homemade bread at the banquet. The private joke in the divine comedy. Your roots.

This, then, is the grandmother's special gift—a bridge to your past. It goes back, of course, to the beginning of time, but I cannot give it substance until my entrance. After all, I am the star.

I arrived with the century but, like the rest of man's history, mine begins with the Fall. I arrived—Helen Hayes Brown did—on the tenth of October, 1900, in Washington, D. C. Center stage, of course. Part of the first harvest, I was in plenty of time for Thanksgiving and looking back on a lifetime filled with the usual quota of pain and guilt and might-have-been, I still offer up a loud hosanna. It's been marvelous. Yes. I came with the century and I believe always in leaving with my escort. It would be nice if it can be managed. I don't want to miss a thing.

Heaven knows my life hasn't always been wise and faultless. It is a pastiche made up of opposites, of lethargy and bossiness, of pride and guilt, of discipline and frivolity. It hasn't always been a model and worthy of imitation, but it was round and it was real and I lived it all greedily.

Your grandmother is an actress who has spent her working life pretending to be gay or sad, hoping that the audience felt the same. More often than not I succeeded. Offstage, I was not always in such control. The technique of living is far more elusive. Alas! One does her best and, like Thornton Wilder's Mrs. Antrobus, I have survived.

Cast by the fates as Helen Hayes, I have played the part

for all it's worth. Child, maiden, sweetheart, wife, and now grandmother. We play many parts in this world and I want you to know them all—for together they make the whole. Trials and errors, hits and misses, I have enjoyed my life, children, and I pray you will, too.

This book is yours, Charlie and Mary; and I leave it in trust for you to be read only when you have reached your maturity. For this is not a fairy story but a tale of grownups who often acted like children, which is quite another thing. It is sometimes called farce and ofttimes tragedy. The combination makes the twin mask which is the symbol of the theatre in which I have spent my years.

And so—in highlights and shadows, bits and pieces, in recalled moments, mad scenes and acts of folly—all chiaroscuro and confetti—this is what it was like to be me, all the me's; what it was like to live in such exciting times and know so many of the men and women who made it so.

> What are little grandchildren made of?
> Some good and some bad from Mother and Dad
> And laughs and wails and Grandmother's tales.

I love you.

GRAMMY

On Reflection

AN AUTOBIOGRAPHY

1

ACTORS cannot choose the manner in which they are born. Consequently, it is the one gesture in their lives completely devoid of self-consciousness.

In reality, one does not always frown with displeasure or grin with delight. Misery and joy are fleeting emotions, often too swift to be captured, caged, and labeled. But the actor must insure audience recognition as well as approval, and there is a language with which he communicates. He is an artist and he is artful. I am afraid that this becomes second nature and it carries over to the actor's life. We search desperately for truth, we actors, and then we improve on it.

In physical torture the actor remembers to look agonized. In ecstasy he quickly becomes wild-eyed with abandon. Even that ultimate moment of truth—the act of dying—can become a farewell performance in the hands of the dedicated who have been known so to extend and postpone a final exit that it becomes truly a cross to be borne by fellow actors and spectators alike.

If this sounds like ridicule, then I must share it. I am an actress and there are times when the superimposition of an emotion has double-exposed the genuine article. Most actors are the same. Relationships, casual or intimate, are frequently played out as they might be in theatre, heightened, dramatized, staged with echoes of past dialogue and gestures that corrupt the spontaneity. Of course, without a prepared script, others do not always react as expected. They don't always pick up their cues. It is then that there is real drama and hell to pay.

We are indeed a strange lot! There are times we doubt that we have any emotions we can honestly call our own. I have approached every dynamic scene change in my life the same way. When I married Charlie MacArthur, I sat down and wondered how I could play the best wife that ever was. I recalled Barrie's Maggie Shand in *What Every Woman Knows*. I had acted her with fine success and decided that my marriage was going to be an even greater triumph. There was no source material too remote, no detail too small—whether observed in others or gleaned from literature—not to be incorporated into the characterization. Heaven knows, I adored Charlie. My love for him was the truest thing in my life; but it was still important that I love him with proper effect, that I *act* loving him with great style, that I achieve the ultimate in wifedom.

I approached maternity in much the same way. The golden fruit of a marriage made in heaven wasn't enough for me. I decided that Whistler's Mother was going to seem like Medea when compared to the perfection of my motherhood. I studied the character and started to draw my portrait—half Olympias and half Mary Cassatt. The mother to mother them all. No matter how real the emotion, the habit of acting is hard to break. If you are a star, then it follows that you must twinkle mightily. There is a price for stardom and, unfortunately, one's family shares in the payment.

By the very nature of my position, I always seem to be center stage, even when I don't wish it. Well, there are worse places to be, and it's a great part. Surely my longest run. But there are occasions when I look at myself in the glass and wonder where the original Helen is—before she was handed the manuscript—the unrehearsed Helen—and then I wonder whether indeed there ever was one.

There must have been a time when I was unquestionably authentic—the real McCoy. Before I started playing my repertoire of roles. How far back can a body go? Through how many stage doors and alleyways and yellowing programs? How do I find the source?

My first recollection. . . . The beginning as I remember it. . . . My mother came home.

*   *   *

I lay in Graddy Hayes's huge bed all propped up with pillows. I was about three years old and so small for my age that, with all of me in it, the bed looked empty still. Shy and quiet, I was called the little white mouse.

My mother was chasing a rainbow and pursuing an acting career with a traveling stock company in a play called *Liberty Belles*. My father, who worked for a wholesale meat company, was selling on the road. Their paths were always to go in different directions and, at this juncture, I was cached with my Grandmother Hayes in Brightwood, outside of Washington, where she kept a Jersey cow.

I had fallen down the back stairs and broken my collar bone, and my reward was to lie in Graddy's bed listening over and over to *Cohen on the Telephone* on the Victrola.

The memory is a warm and cozy one made truly perfect by its finish. Mother returned from her gallivanting and took me home. Mother's returns were the high spots of my childhood. I know now that she had to have her whirl. Dissatisfied with her pedestrian life, she was having her last fling.

This was made possible by years of scrimping. She had saved enough money to study acting at the Robert Downey School, where she met a girl whose husband had the most tenuous of theatrical connections. Eventually, through her she landed a job with Fred Burger, who ran a third-rate touring company. His wife Bess was the leading woman and Mother was the comedienne. It was the most feckless and spasmodic of enterprises and Mother was continually coming and going. I remember vividly the horror I always felt on her leaving and the wonder of her return.

Everything brightened when Mother came home, and Father and I were gloriously happy. There was great laughter again. It was up and down with Mother. When she was up, there was no more delightful creature, and one forgot the bad times.

Her tour in *Liberty Belles* was hardly a triumphant one, and she entertained the family with hilarious tales of her experiences when she returned. Once, in a southern hotel, in order to avoid paying the bill, Fred had to divert the desk clerk with a long harangue on the need for more bath towels, while Mother and Bess tiptoed down the stairs and into the alleyway with their bags. Mother's re-enacting of the scene —her stealthy walking-on-eggshells imitation—gave the classically shabby story such suspense that one wondered if the girls made it or were caught. But then she'd skip off to freedom, her tongue mischievously between her teeth, a glint in her eye, and everyone would shriek with laughter.

Mother could make the most marvelous faces. She could

lift one corner of her mouth clear up to her nose—making a harelip—and cross her eyes at the same time. This was her specialty. The effect was staggeringly funny and it was for years my great ambition to be able to accomplish this. I never could.

With her irrepressible if spasmodic merriment, Mother would turn her back on her audience in *Liberty Belles* and break up the other members of the cast with this special talent. Fred Burger always threatened to fire her, but found her as irresistible as everyone else did. Obviously a serious actress, she was frank enough to tell anything at all about herself if it made a good story.

It seems that when the little company played New Haven, many of the Yale boys, no doubt as a form of criticism and in order to pep up the proceedings, jumped onto the stage, taking over the plot and the heroine. They picked up Bess and spun her around, passing her from one to the other in a mad rigadoon. Fred stood in the back of the half-empty theatre, torn between husbandly distress and managerial gratitude that the paying customers were at last having a good time. Mother made his dilemma hysterically funny in the telling. She found humor everywhere—except in the tiny world where her drab marriage and dreary motherhood had trapped her.

Tempestuous and bitter, Mother would fly into tantrums, followed by days of brooding silence that would leave Father and me bewildered and wretched. Wildly romantic notions kept her going in circles, refusing to accept the facts of her life.

❋　❋　❋

In those days, grandmothers were always available for extra duties, so Graddy looms large in the first scenes of my childhood. Everything about Graddy Hayes was warm and safe and loving. She was the last of the generation of real grandmothers. One of the women who made a special grace of age.

Unthinkable as it would be to the eternal soubrettes of today, there was once a breed of women who by their mid-50s admitted that youth was a sweet memory. After a long, wistful sigh, they willingly moved on to the next step in their development. And they dressed the part. They didn't defy the seasons of woman, and greying hair softened their worn faces. They didn't lose their full-blown beauty in an effort to freeze its first bloom. Dark or quiet colors in dress were further reminders of a new-found stability. They didn't compete with their daughters but, instead, presented a contrast that illustrated the logical sequence of life. There was flow and a natural progression.

I know that Faust and several of my friends have sold their souls for a reprise of youth. I know, too, that all the sciences are properly committed to a slowing down of the aging process. Certainly, the lengthening of the productive years and the husbanding of health and energy are not to be dismissed. I am also not without my vanities. But what a silly world we would live in with no one but the eternally young dashing about, being passionate about everything and impatient with everybody else. And how tragic to die young. There is a cycle; and I hate halfway measures. My Graddy Hayes wore long, full skirts that made a comfortable lap to sit in; her rocking chair was a cradle. Grandmothers didn't go in and out a great deal in those days. She seemed always to be there when I needed her. When she did venture down the street, her feathered bonnet tied with ribbons under one ear was the only residual sign of girlish vanity, and it was a delight, like the last leaf on a tree in winter.

On a Saturday night, Graddy would take me to the Star Nickelodeon to see Broncho Billy or Florence Turner and

Maurice Costello, and I would be allowed to tie the bow under her hat and straighten the coral pin that held the white ruching at her throat. How important it made me feel to see that she was properly turned out. Graddy always lost one glove, and so—as long as I could remember—she wore one and carried another, since they were never mates. It gave her real dash, I thought. When she regaled the family with a scene-by-scene description of what we'd witnessed at the movies, I was treated to a glorious bonus. What a performance! She had a great gift for mimickry, and the entire family would lie around enjoying the whole show for the price of two seats.

Graddy Hayes could do no wrong in any department. She might have been leary of our Chapin Street wall telephone with the crank, but Graddy had powers to receive messages without such newfangled machinery. Where her family was concerned, Graddy Hayes could always sense trouble brewing. In her active years, she would suddenly cock her fine head as if she were heeding some distant bell and then she'd hurriedly dress for outdoors with the announcement, "I'll be at Maggie's," or "Lizzie isn't well," or "Your cousin Thelma is sick and Mamie needs me." And she'd be off answering the call.

Graddy Hayes was a good woman and a devout Catholic, but easy in her faith. On intimate terms with God, she dispensed with many of the formalities. My grandfather, Patrick, treated the Lord like an ineffectual partner who, in His infinite mercy, didn't know how to run the business. To Patrick Hayes, however, the smallest omission in ritual demanded divine rage.

According to Mother, and I can't swear it's gospel, her father's love of reading was so great that he was compelled to pick up scraps of paper anywhere he found them, if they had even one line of print. Once wound up on this topic,

Mother would insist that—after a couple of whiskies—Patrick Hayes could do any scene from Shakespeare by heart, playing all the parts. This, of course, was sheer invention. I suspect that the old man—in his cups—might *once* have commanded the attention of his frightened family with a loud, "Tibee or not tibee, is it now? 'Tis the question I'd be askin'!" I knew my imaginative mother. I also knew the background that she felt required to embroider for the family picture.

It is true that my grandfather was the nephew of Catherine Hayes—the Swan of Erin, as she was known. Catherine was a singer beloved throughout the Emerald Isle and the toast of London when she appeared at the Albert Hall. She became a great favorite of the '49ers in California when she toured America, no doubt to find her own gold in the streets. Surely, she did achieve celebrity, and I actually have a picture of her on some sheet music which she made popular. The song was *John Anderson My Jo* with words by Bobby Burns. Mother never quite recovered from the blow when she heard that Catherine had wanted to adopt her father when she was at the height of her fame. Mother was sure that he would have become world renowned at something or other, thereby opening the portals of international society to her. She never quite forgave the family, who wouldn't allow it because the Swan was a renegade and a Protestant, and giving the child over to her would certainly have sealed his eternal doom.

*   *   *

Whatever charms young Patrick had had to engage the pert singer's interest were long since dissipated. The old man was a fanatic who drove one son to the bottle and an early grave, several daughters to early marriage, and Graddy to the cookie jar to steal nickels in order to escape his austerity. She fled into the beauty of theatre; with her stagestruck Essie—my mother, Catherine Estelle.

After Grandfather lost his sight and earning power, there were times when money was so scarce that Graddy couldn't afford fish on Friday. Disguising leftovers with a cream sauce or heightening bland vegetables with some of yesterday's beef gravy, Graddy tried to make do. But after he had said Grace, Patrick Hayes would lift the platter to his nose. Squinting suspiciously, he evidently sniffed fire and brimstone. "Flesh!" he would shout—with which religious observation he would then send the platter, dishes, and food flying across the room.

Many were the times his sons and daughters ate off Graddy's floor. And they could. Graddy's fingers were practically skinless from the yellow lye soap that she used to wash and scrub. Ads and commercials notwithstanding, Graddy Hayes' red, rough hands were beautiful memories of my childhood. Whenever she stayed with us, I loved being near her and would watch while she embroidered the most startling cushion covers. I remember particularly a head of Lincoln in raw silk on linen. But her *chef-d'oeuvre* was the Irish flag and Old Glory with crossed staffs intertwined with shamrocks and goldenrod. Above and below were the mottos *E Pluribus Unum* and *Erin Go Bragh*. This one was the height of her handiwork and far too lofty for the bottoms of the likes of us. It was never sat on but framed and hung in the living room.

When alone with her embroidery, Graddy would sit near the window, the grey light bathing her like a Gaelic Vermeer, and she would mumble and frown and then smile to herself. One could almost see the memories like stereopticon slides, each exacting its own reaction and then being replaced by the next. Sometimes Graddy's grey eyes would wrinkle more than ever and she would laugh out loud. This was the cue I would wait for.

"What is it, Graddy? What's so funny?"

"Go back to your homework, child, or your mother won't let you go out and play after supper."

"I don't care. I'd rather hear what made you laugh." And it was true.

"Helen Hayes Brown," Graddy would intone, the deliberate pronunciation of my name labeling me an arch criminal far beyond redemption. "Tsk! Tsk!" But her recovery was miraculous. "Honestly, Helen—oh, well!"

And we were off on a marvelous trip into her past. I paid my passage, all right, by extracting the pesky raw silk from the skeins because her hands were so rough that she was always in danger of tangling the knot. I've since wondered if my Graddy didn't have a touch of perfidy. That chuckle could easily have been a lure. But no matter, her stories were shared moments of love. They became part of my life, those souvenirs of her youth in England.

Graddy actually saw a youngish Victoria, still a happy wife, dressed in blue, riding in her carriage with her Albert at her side, and waving her plump hand. She actually heard gossip of royal romances. How those high and mighty carried on—the scandals!—and how respectable they all sound now, with changes of values and the old Queen gone. All that purple dust. How those tasty morsels must have been passed around and been gasped over and savored with tea around the kitchen table in Liverpool.

Of course, I didn't know what it all meant anyway, and the only shockers to me were Graddy's scarey tales of ghosts and supernatural goings-on. I always shivered and thrilled to the one about the beautiful bride who expired of a mysterious seizure in the arms of her groom just as the priest was declaring them man and wife. Shrouded in her own wedding gown, fairly floating in her many veils, the virgin was transported to her grave. Followed by a long procession of weeping mourners, she lay in a hearse pulled by fine black horses, each with three white plumes. As the carriage passed through the cemetery gate, it rolled over a sharp rock and the jolt was so great that up shot the lid of the coffin. The bride's eyes and hands started to flutter; and then sitting up in bewilderment, her pale lips formed those deathless words, "Where am I?" The horrified cortege dispersed in panic—all except the bridegroom, of course, who now lifted her tenderly in his arms, brought the color back to her cheeks with a kiss, and carried her off to their marriage bed.

This story and my grandmother's insistence that it wasn't really unusual—"People, Helen, are being buried alive *all* the time!"—made such an impression on me that when she herself lay in her coffin a few years later and at the age of ten I looked upon a dead person for the first time, I of course wailed, "Sit up, Graddy. Please sit up *now!*"

Graddy's friends sat clutching their wrists, their necks pulled in like great turtles, their mouths twisted in scandalized disbelief.

"Well, I *never.*"

"What a little actress!"

"Essie, you shouldn't allow her to show off like that."

They were the first of a legion of critics who have tried to remove me from the stage.

I really was sure that, like the pop-up bride, she would rise and spin a yarn about this, her latest adventure. The finality of death was beyond me. I just couldn't believe that my Graddy was gone.

*　*　*

I would lie with my school book on the floor praying for one of Graddy's monologues. The best were those about the family, about my aunts and uncles when children, and about my mother's pretensions, which were eventually to have such a positive effect on my life.

The Hayeses were scamp Irish. There are the careful, thrifty Irish and there are the other kind. We were the other kind. But Mother, even as a child, dreamed of something else. She tried to find it in the rotogravure section of the Sunday pages, where she lapped up every bit of information she could concerning the cream of society. Life was a drawing-room comedy to my mother, and she felt she had been relegated to the kitchen.

I was even named for Helen Gould, one of the leading socialites of the day and a model of elegance and tone to my mother. How painful it must have been for her during those early years at home with the menfolk sitting collarless and the other girls deaf to her snooty shenanigans. How displaced she must have felt. Only Graddy understood.

"I remember the time," Graddy mused, one of those pearl-grey afternoons so long ago, "that Essie took a notion she couldn't drink morning coffee." Graddy took a deep breath. She was going to need it, bless her. "That's right, child. She just couldn't drink her morning coffee. She was working at Criswell's Drugstore as cashier, your mother being the first of my girls to want to go out and work, and Pat and me not liking it; but your grandfather's sight was gone already and I was on his job in the Department of the Interior. Well, I had to be at work at eight, which meant I'd be leaving the house by seven, the horsecars being so unreliable, and it would be six o'clock when I'd be getting the breakfast for all the wage-earners. Lizzie and Maggie were already married and Mamie was having callers and helping with the house except in the mornings—she just couldn't get herself up in the morning. Then there was Ben and Tom before he died, poor boy, from the consumption, and Frank and Essie, your Ma and me. Of course, Pat would be there only to make sure that we'd be saying Grace—a real stickler he was—or didn't have any ham on a Friday, as if we could afford it often—or the children weren't doing any swearing or disrespect and all, or shipping everybody off to Mass. Well now, one morning like a bolt from the blue, Essie decides she's not drinking coffee for breakfast any more but only after supper, which she's calling 'dinner' now—supper being what they were having at the fancy restaurants after the theatre. My Essie, your ma, decided that it was the thing to be drinking tea now in the morning. Well, the boys started teasing and Pat started sputtering, but there was nothing in the Bible that said a body *had* to drink coffee in the morning, so there we were. Oh, the teasing! Ben and Tom were just tormenting her with things like 'Well, Faith, if Lady Veer Deveer ain't been readin' the sassiety news again." And 'Ain't she the hoity toity one? She'll be asking us all to dress up in evening clothes to have our breakfast porridge.' And the like. Oh, they were something—and now and then they'd remind her of how much more work it was for me. But I didn't care because I knew that Essie was reaching out the only way she knew to improve her position in life, and she didn't have many ways of improving in our house, I'll tell you, and if a bit of tea on waking up to the awful day helped her—anyway, I started noticing that she wasn't finishing that tea once she was having her way, and though the bunch of them had stopped deviling her with their mock, I noticed that she was sniffing greedily at Pat's coffee, which was next to her, sitting so near him she was; and I wondered about it and thought it was about time I helped her out of the fix she was in of her own doing—*so* the next morning I poured her a cup of coffee in the kitchen, put in a real lot of milk and sugar, and took it in and set it before her. 'Essie,' said I, 'I'd like you to taste the new drink from Paris, France, that

Mr. Haring at the market was telling me about. It's called *café,* and all the great ladies and gentlemen are drinking it like crazy over there in the grand cafés, which are named for the libation.' Well, Essie—so grateful—took a sip, took some more, rolled it around on her palate a bit, and her eyes lighted up like stars they did. She drank it down in a single gulp. And that was the end of the tea business, I'm tellin' you."

And so I was able to meet my mother as a young girl and a silly goose and be comforted by the revelation. I was also able to know my wonderful Graddy Hayes as that paradox of paradoxes—an Irish diplomat. Graddy, it is plain to see, could be a non-stop talker, and so could Mother. My mother made Graddy sound taciturn, and my Charlie made them both sound like mutes. I have lived most of my life with monologuists, unable to get a word in edgewise, but I have had my inning and have long since made up for my days of silence.

2

How enchanting my mother was. She was so gay and so effervescent. But only after many years and much growing up did I recognize the pressures that created that bubbling personality.

Her marriage did not provide the escape she had hoped for but simply replaced one set of bars with another, and my arrival on the scene must really have sounded the death knell to her fantasy life.

Closing her ears she fled, and I was unloaded onto her best friend, Annie Hess (my godmother) or Graddy. Annie was a good plain German spinster girl, who—along with Graddy and Aunt Mamie—created the sweet-smelling, warm, safe world I inhabited those first years when Brownie was trying to become an actress.

Aunt Mamie loved her drink and me more than anything else in the world. Though she had two children of her own, she was always making me clothes and fussing over me. She had inherited Graddy's skill with a needle but none of her style, so my wardrobe was completely outlandish. Mother dreamed we were Vanderbilts, and darling Aunt Mamie decked me out like Mrs. Astor's pet horse. I believe that she thought me a doll to be dressed and played with. My visits with her and cousins Thelma and Ruel were always a joy to me. When Mother was home, Aunt Mamie was never far away. Almost nightly she would arrive with paper containers of ice cream and some more fabric to drape around me.

Annie Hess's house was another of my homes. It was never without the wonderful smell of strudels and pancakes. Those groaning boards! But it was the same in all the houses, that feeling of opulence so rarely displayed by the rich.

Only after the adults had full bellies and their belts and stays were loosened did the children eat. The table was now laid for a second sitting—just like a luxury liner. Children were seen and not heard in those days, and we would pant for food while the grownups gorged themselves. Unlike today's very young, who teeter uncomfortably on the pinnacle of power, we knew our places and scrambled to them gratefully when we were at last beckoned. Stuffed with food, we would then play games. Fantan played with matchsticks was a favorite at Aunt Mamie's.

It was a lovely world of warmth and continuity. Middle class, close knit, and hard working. Everyone seemed to love being together. Kitchens were always turning out wonders and borning rooms creating new cousins. A sick aunt or widowed grandmother rarely ended up a public charge, but became part of a household, a fixture. There was always room for one more. No one ached to lead his own life, except poor Mother.

I remember sprawling, apple-cheeked children and chattering women with aprons, bustling in cozy, cooking-sweet rooms, tending their menfolk. There was such a clutter of hooked rugs and samplers and copper pots. Everything was always being used and then cleaned and used again. Nothing ever sat, especially the women. The rooms were alive and the energy spilled from one part of the house to another in a never-ending rush of giving. What a sense of belonging —even if you didn't quite. And when Mother would come home, the picture was complete.

It all seemed like one long holiday. The faintest whiff of pine or peppermint and I am carried back to the most wonderful times of all, those first and best of Christmases. Preparations would start in November. Father and I and the Brown cousins and the Hayeses, too, would all go into the woods to hunt black walnuts, and we must sometimes have invaded private property because I recall being chased by cows. Then we would all run for cover. But these brute caretakers didn't keep us from filling flour sacks to brimming before we returned home. Those fat sacks would sit until the beginning of December and then Graddy or Aunt Mamie would open them and start the happy business of candymaking.

The walnuts were placed on a long wooden table and two large flatirons were used to crush them. The banging was deafening. When it was over and the poor nuts lay mutilated, we children were employed to pick the meat out of the broken pieces and transfer the golden bits into waiting bowls. Filling the bowls seemed an impossible labor—the particles were so small—but laboring together as we did, all the work added up and eventually we would see results. Encouraged, we would raise the level even higher.

The fondant was made in a great cauldron, and as it would bubble, we small ones would circle it like sweet-toothed, salivating Druids. The sweetmeats were put aside to set for a week. There was this one made of black walnut; one of strawberry; and another of chocolate. The bonbons were waiting to be made, and the children were allowed to join in the chocolate dipping. We always ended up covered from head to toe—frenzied, giggling confections.

This was the beginning of the Christmas planning. We were now given reams of paper, scissors, and pots of home-made paste. Our job was to make the traditional colored-paper chains for decorations. Then there was popcorn-stringing and after that was over, we all settled down—Sissie and Lottie Brown and George and Thelma and Ruel and all the cousins—to make our gifts: terrible tie racks with Indian heads and cedar boxes with awful designs. My poor uncles and aunts! Out of Christian charity they were forced to use these monstrosities which we created in an atmosphere of keen competition. But even the good gifts, given to us by the grownups, were homemade. These were usually beauti-ful, though the materials never cost more than a dollar and a half. Anyway, by the time the tree was dressed, the apples hung on branches to weight them, the boxes placed at its base, it was really Christmas—and the like of it will not come again.

Mother's participation in the celebration was sentimental and not religious. Rebelling against her sanctimonious father, Mother turned away from the Church altogether. Would that we were wise enough to make our choices rationally, instead of in imitation or fierce reaction. But so goes the never-ending game of the generations back to God knows when.

The last place in the world one would expect Mother to have sent me was a Catholic school, but destiny was at work, and that's where I landed. Mother's prejudices were ex-ceeded only by her fear of vaccination. The law was clear. All children enrolling in public schools had to be vaccinated against smallpox. Tales of horror had reached my mother's ears—canards of arms and legs eaten away by the poisoned pinpricks and the injection of disease. She declared that only over her dead body would I be so mutilated. This resistance to the new was uncharacteristic of Mother. But it led me to the Church she had turned her back on. Distrust of the needle gave her no choice. Holy Cross made no such demand. I presume this was because it was not under the jurisdiction of the Board of Education and not because faith was sufficient protection.

It was this strange and happy happenstance that landed me at Holy Cross Academy when it was time for me to go to school. This was when the forces beyond control started working. Not only was I exposed to the Faith which now sustains me, but I was simultaneously introduced to the wonders of the theatre. Nuns are great theatre buffs, and Holy Cross Academy was humming with theatricals. I made my first appearance there as Peaseblossom in *Midsummer Night's Dream*. It was also at Holy Cross that I first fell in love with the Sisters and dreamed of becoming a nun. The closest I ever got to that goal was playing *White Sister* with Clark Gable in that latter-day Gomorrah, Hollywood. But as a child at Holy Cross and later at Sacred Heart, I was fascinated with the glamor and dedication of the nuns, swept up in the beauty of the story of Jesus. It was so wondrously presented to a child's heart. I was devoted to my prayers. I wore out all the knees of my stockings with my constant praying. Mother had saved me from the needle and now she was stuck with the alternative. Mother! Catherine Estelle Hayes Brown!

Years later when I told Edward Sheldon, Charlie's collaborator on *Salvation Nell*, that I was a renegade Catholic, he said, "You'll go back to the Church, Helen. Catholics never stay away forever, and anyway I think all actors should be Catholics. Of all the faiths, Catholicism has the most

drama and color and music. It's really the actor's religion,"
was his conclusion.

* * *

I wish Grandmother Brown had been as communicative
as Graddy Hayes. I should love to have known Francis Van
Arnum Brown before he grew up to be my father. But then
—he never did grow up really. He never deserted his boyhood but remained content with the tiniest successes.
Mother chose the least aggressive of the five Brown brothers
as her own. He married for love of the spirited and witty
Irish girl, against his mother's wishes. Grandma Brown, sitting fat in her middle-class eminence, would never bend to
her daughter-in-law or her family. As the young couple settled down to living together it must have been plain to all
that two less likely mates could not be imagined. He married
for love and a home; she married for escape from home. He
wanted peace; she wanted freedom. The young Browns were
at odds from the start, and when I came along I only made
matters worse.

Unlike the Irish immigrants who were the Hayeses, the
Browns had come to America when it was still a crown
colony. Although they never became rich, they prospered
and helped create the solid, dependable middle class that
has always been our backbone. No history of poverty spurred
my father to heights of industry. In his blood there was no
Swan of Erin singing of fame and fortune. With none of the
waywardness, volatility, or imagination the Hayeses had to
brimming, Father took the world as he found it and relished
what was in his reach. His easy satisfaction was both his
curse and blessing.

Fat and jolly, adored by all children, Father could imitate
the sound of birds and dogs and cows grazing. He liked
people, and selling for a meat and poultry company made it

possible for him to spend a lot of time with them. At leisure
he was pleased to labor in his garden, making things grow
the way his own father had. Highlights of his life were trips
to the bandstand near the Washington Monument where
we'd watch John Philip Sousa conduct the U. S. Marine
Band in his wonderful red, white, and blue marches—or to
nearby Glen Echo Amusement Park's ferris wheel—or out to
the ball park.

When Mother was playing bridge with her friends, Father
often took me on Sundays to watch his errant Washington
Senators and worship his god, Walter Johnson, the greatest
pitcher ever to walk on a field, according to Father. While I
happily munched away at peanuts and popcorn and Cracker
Jack and watched some baseball clowns hired by the Senators to entertain us, I would be dazed by a running commen-
tary. We must have been a picture: the two of us, this round,
excited, straw-hatted baseball fan and the tiny, nodding
child, commiserating with him that this genius of the mound,
his Walter Johnson, was stuck with a team that just wasn't
in the same league he was in. Walter Johnson! I knew everything about him inside and out.

Mother would have been mortified at the ball park, if ever
she'd come with us. My dear, quiet father changed completely the minute we got to the bleachers. All tranquility
left him and he became a rooter. Cupping his hands to his
mouth, he shouted instructions to the home team and south-
erly directions to the visitors. I'm afraid Father was a character in the bleachers. I would cringe as the delighted crowd—
either in total agreement with his judgment or simply to
encourage his shenanigans—would yell, "That's telling him,
Fat Boy!" or "Give 'em hell, Fatty!" Encouraged to be louder
and funnier, Father, utterly released, would dream up some
topper like, "What do you mean, 'Ball One?' You're as blind
as that bat!"

The crowd around us would go wild with appreciation, and I would be so embarrassed that I'd shrink lower and lower on the bench till one day I almost fell under the man behind me. Daddy, blindly in love with Johnson, just continued screaming. This was his ball field and it was a world which he understood. He knew whom he was for and whom he was against. And he let them know it. When we went home, he was himself again. The gentlest, kindest, dearest man who ever lived.

I loved the trips with Father to Rock Creek Park to search for the first arbutus in late winter on one of those wild March days. We would forage around beneath the dried leaves of the previous fall until we would find one of these signs of rebirth.

Those tough little plants have to push their way through the frost; they are impossible to dislodge simply by pulling. Father would get out his old penknife and delicately cut around the roots to remove them. At day's end, we would wend our happy way home with nosegays of the tiny fragrant stars. Discovering spring with my father was a seasonal rite. In recall, those March breezes still cling to my cheeks. I become buoyant with the lightness of heart I used to have as we wandered through the dappled light of the woods in our quest. I was his girl, all right, all right, and we made lovely memories.

❋   ❋   ❋

I was still under five years old when Mother found me in our four-legged tub with a towel draped around my head and waving one of those rattan fans with the painted pictures that we used in Washington, D. C., in those hot, pre-air-conditioned summers.

"And who do you think *you* are, Darling?" Mother asked, picking up the Fairy soap.

Now all children love to pretend, and any number of them might have responded as I did. I had seen a painting in a gallery and had asked who the naked lady was, surrounded by so many adoring friends. Mother had read the title aloud. I was much impressed, and now lay in the tub impressing myself.

"I'm Clee O'Patrick in her bath!" I answered grandly. Well, the significance that Mother attached to this bit of pretense was wholly disproportionate to the fact. The whole family was informed that a new Bernhardt was in the works, though not quite dry behind the ears.

When Mother asked me—after I was at Holy Cross a while —what musical instrument I wanted to study, I answered, "The hark," immediately. More devout than the Mother Superior herself and apparently arranging my own apotheosis, I visualized myself an angel—sitting on a cloud—playing celestial music to the delight of my betters. Since I was about 12 inches tall at the time and might just as well have tried to negotiate a cello, Mother thought the violin might be more practical. Misunderstanding my fantasy for great interest in music, she persuaded my father that I must study seriously and with the best of equipment.

In what was later to be called a pincer movement, she now enrolled me at Miss Minnie Hawke's School of Dance—to teach me the poise she so admired in the town's leading debutantes—and simultaneously bought me a tiny violin. Father no doubt balked at the Stradivarius that Mother, with characteristic zeal, must have demanded. Whether it was to be Sarah Bernhardt or Fritz Kreisler, Mother was going to make either or both possible. She was blindly following the path that was laid out for us.

With Catherine Hayes lurking in my past and Mother now seeing to my future, my destiny seemed assured. Something more was added to her desire to be cultured, to be social, to be a great lady. Something more led her to the concert hall, the art gallery, and the opera house, as well as the legitimate theatre.

Some of these places she later even learned to enjoy. It is to her eternal credit that she went to them before she had learned how. The reasons may have been wrong but the instinct was right. I suppose if the Vanderbilts and Goulds and Astors had spent their days in the pool hall, I would have spent my life picking up a completely different set of cues. But they didn't. And the refinements and delicacies of the leisure class seeped down to what my darling mother would never admit was wild, scamp, working-class Irish.

Just as Graddy had loved the theatre and had bought stale vegetables and second-cut meats in order to afford gallery seats, now Mother introduced me to the greats. There was a difference, though. Graddy was enriching her life. Mother was out to change hers—and mine.

When the lights dimmed in the theatre, all that was ugly and crowding and oppressive was blacked out for Mother. She was one with the ladies in the boxes, and those on stage. To sit in the peanut gallery, we had to get to the box office early in order to buy the unreserved 25¢ perches that were called "rush-seats." They were well named. We would wait on line for hours, and when the doors opened, we would rush up four long flights of stairs, mobs of theatre-lovers pushing each other aside in their uphill race to the best of the worst seats. One had to be healthy to be in the competition. If not, running those three flights of stairs at a dead heat would have been hazardous sport.

Small, nimble, and slippery, I darted like a goldfish through a sea of legs and invective. When I reached the top I would fling myself across two first row seats staking my claim until Mother, carried along with the tide, found me. Excrutiatingly shy, I would clutch the two seats with whitening knuckles and stiffening toes, my lips a thin determined line, my eyes tight shut to avoid the sharp glances of the outraged losers. But I held the hard-earned territory until relief arrived. I would then return to character and sit quietly while Mother would read the program aloud and chatter about the new fashions on the ladies in the boxes below. Mother was never at a loss for words, and I was just the best listener that ever was.

What a delightful companion Mother was! She had a way of lighting up the sky with all her enthusiasms, and when she decided that I was special, we became gay traveling companions. We now shared everything from Paderewski to Huyler's chocolates.

When Forbes-Robertson played *Hamlet* in Washington, Mother and I made our pilgrimage. We started waiting in line at eight a.m. for our rush-seats. Once again safely ensconced in our perches, I was utterly baffled as the Melancholy Dane rambled on.

"What's it mean, Mother?"

"Do be *quiet!*"

"But I don't underst——"

It was then that a cultivated voice whispered in my ear.

"He's wondering if he should live or die—unhappy with one, afraid of the other."

I turned and saw a Negro gentleman. Not allowed to sit in the orchestra of the house, though he could obviously afford it, he was my first guide to Shakespeare. As the play unfolded, he provided me with a simple, quiet explanation. On stage, the razor-sharp Forbes-Robertson cut quite a magnificent figure as the Prince but it was the man beside me who made memorable a play I shouldn't have been seeing in the first place.

The Merry Widow was less of a strain on my intellect, although it did stimulate my imagination. Donald Brian and

Lina Abarbanell were Prince Danilo and Sonia, the very
symbols of romantic love to me. There was some bond twixt
these two beautiful people. Some mysterious thing was going
on between them. That man wanted something from that
woman and I didn't know what. I thought about it a great
deal for a while and then filed the pleasant problem away as
I met the next new challenge.

No great artist appeared in Washington whom I didn't
see. When Mischa Elman was scheduled to play, we went off
once more to the heights. Mother still thought that the violin
might be my career, though I had shown but the slightest
proclivity toward it. She was still trying to convince Daddy
to pay for lessons. During the concert, she noticed a new
shine in my eyes, a new glow on my face. She brought me
home on a wave of new enthusiasm.

"Frank Brown!" She began smugly. "I want you to take a
good look at your daughter."

"Essie . . ." my father tried to interrupt.

"We just heard Elman—*Mischa Elman*—and look at her.
She's transported!"

"Essie . . ."

"I told you she had music in her soul. How many children
at her age would be so exhilarated by great music that they'd
be practically in a fever? Did you ever see her eyes that
bright?"

"Never!" my father admitted. "And look at her neck—she's
got the measles!"

It was true. And Mother always told the story on herself.
I'll give her that. But it didn't stop her from trying—again
and again. My poor father. There were forces at work, and,
as with my mother, they were out of his control.

❋   ❋   ❋

Who would have thought that it would be Miss Minnie

Hawke and her sister, Miss May, those top-heavy little women who used to drive up F Avenue in their electric brougham, who would point the direction and send me on my way?

On occasion they used to show off their little rich pupils in theatricals, and once a year the Hawke sisters with all their mighty connections gave a "May Ball" for charity at the Belasco Theater.

The first season I had skipped onto the stage to do an Irish reel in a green satin dress with spangled shamrocks. Each was meticulously sewed on by Aunt Mamie. I skipped onto that stage and skipped off so quickly that neither the shamrocks nor I could be seen. Through sheer stage fright I couldn't remember anything beyond the skipping circle which began all of Miss Minnie Hawke's dances. It was my only case of such fright, and it was clear that I was not meant to be a dancer.

When the second year's performance was being planned, Miss Hawke felt that, lest I discourage future dance pupils with another such fiasco, I return instead to song.

I had once done one that had pleased her. It was about the Zuyder Zee and I was all decked out in a peasant costume and lace cap. Mother had directed me to sob a little when I sang of my sweetheart who had gone off to America. She had even suggested that, since a bit of nose-running always accompanied my crying, I might use the hem of the apron as a handkerchief when I was through. It was a howling success.

Now Miss Minnie insisted that I do another such number. For the occasion Mother rehearsed me in an impersonation of Annabelle Whitford doing her "Gibson Girl Bathing Beauty" turn from the *Ziegfeld Follies*. I wore a sleeveless black taffeta suit with absurd decolleté made by Aunt Mamie, and my hair was piled high with a puff Mother had picked up at the five and dime. In an extremely bored manner, I sang:

> Why do they call me the Gibson Girl
> The Gibson Girl
> The Gibson Girl
> What is the matter with Mr. Ibsen
> Why Dana Gibson?
> Just wear a blank expression
> And a monumental curl
> Walk with a bend in your back and
> They'll call you the Gibson Girl.

Lew Fields of the famous Weber and Fields was playing in Washington that week in a musical called *It Happened in Nordland,* and he had lent Miss Hawke some scenery. In a questionable matching of generosity, Miss Minnie invited the Dutch comic to the matinee. He was not playing that afternoon and—amazingly enough—he arrived. I must have struck him funny because he wrote the manager of the theatre that, if and when my parents were interested in a stage career for me once I was older, he wanted to be first in line. One of my parents was *very* interested. But New York was a long way off. I was five years old!

That summer, Fred Burger, the producer of *Liberty Belles,* was running a local stock company called The Columbia Players, and he needed a child for *The Prince Chap.* He agreed to give Mother a role if she would allow me to play the lead. And so I made my debut with Mother.

These years are very misty, but I do remember Mother's doing a death scene that was terrifying. I remember being further disturbed when I noticed that the poverty-stricken character she was playing was wearing silken hose.

Father's fellow Elks, the students at Holy Cross, and Mother's bridge club—all eager to see little Helen Brown—

made business boom for the Columbia Players, establishing me, at once, as a box-office draw.

Fred Burger now put on two plays a summer in which I could appear. In the first few years I played *Mrs. Wiggs of the Cabbage Patch, The Prince and the Pauper,* and *Little Lord Fauntleroy.*

What is so glad-making about this is that Graddy was able to see me in the theatre—although she was far from my favorite audience. I would hear as counterpoint to my dialogue such comments as "She was always funny around the house," if the moment were amusing, or "She was always a sensitive child," if the scene were a tearjerker.

Though Father raised his eyebrows at all this activity, he did—as a proud papa—want me to appear along with all his fellow Elks' children at some big "do." Mother wouldn't allow it. She considered me a professional. She now had her sights set on New York, though one would have thought it was Paris from the extra French lessons I took that year in preparation for a career. Brownie had decided I was going to be a great lady, and, obviously, great ladies spoke French. Mother was always concerned with what was ladylike and what wasn't. She was so wayward, my mother. She made the best fried chicken and lemon meringue pie imaginable but would never teach me to cook. Memories of Graddy's life would always haunt her. "You're not going to be a slavie, Helen." But Mother worked harder than any slave to take us where we were going. She washed lace curtains to pay a tutor to round out what she believed to be an incomplete French curriculum at Sacred Heart. Mademoiselle Peletier—a friend of hers—was governess to an ambassador's children. She saw me on her day off.

I would catch the streetcar and go down Connecticut Avenue to the imposing Wickfeld Mansion. Standing in front of it with a fresh satin bow in my hair, I looked for all the world like a Ronald Searle illustration. The butler would scowlingly answer the door and lead me through an immense marble reception hallway with a sweeping staircase; and then I would be enclosed in the first elevator I'd ever seen and would float up to the servants' quarters on the top floor.

Mademoiselle would greet me in hushed tones that made her exquisite Parisian accent even more difficult to understand. Our lessons were supposedly quite secretive, and I don't know who this child was supposed to be who arrived on the dot of three every Thursday. With all that pussy-footing and our rendezvous in the nearby park on fine days— chattering away in a foreign tongue—one could have thought us spies.

That gorgeous house! Once I saw the owner in a long, beautiful dressing gown draped across the shining bannister on one of the landings. She was so regal and so langorous— the quintessence of Mother's "Lady."

I trembled at the sight of such grandeur; and then she yelled "Alex!" in a grating voice that should have been asking who put the overalls in Mrs. Murphy's chowder. It was the voice of a fishwife and not meant to be heard by a stranger. I will never forget that, frightened as I felt, I was ever so grateful that I was not Alex or—as my instructor instructed me to say it—*son mari*.

Well! Mother's *mari, mon père,* was bewildered by developments. His women no longer belonged to him, but it was Papa who paid all the way. Mother prevailed upon him to buy us our fare to Gotham to try our luck.

"After all, Lew Fields *said* he was interested in Helen!"

In New York, we sat outside his door for hours that first time, and when Mr. Fields came out of his sanctum with the beautiful Lotta Faust, Mother waited for him to escort the actress through the swinging door of the office. On his return she thrust a photograph of me as the little bathing beauty into his face.

"You do remember Helen, don't you, Mr. Fields?"

It was more a declaration than a question. Mother had no doubts. Mother was right. I was signed that afternoon to play little Mimi in his fall production of *Old Dutch.*

"You see, Frank? Those train tickets *were* the best investment you ever made!"

She was wild Irish, Mother was, and my father a stolid, earthbound darling. He was the most successful man I ever knew and his sweetness of nature insured his worldly failure. In harmony with the world, he was in perpetual discord with his restless wife. He was dear and I adored him, but I can quite understand how enraging his passivity must have been to the seething woman who was my mother.

My father smilingly led me down a knoll to spy the first arbutus peep through the ground. My mother propelled me up to the gallery to see Nijinski leap in the air.

I was the only thing that my parents ever had in common. They were born antagonists, but I thank heaven for their misalliance.

3

THAT's how it all began. Mother searching for fulfillment put me on the stage. Father, incapable of discord, ironically kept me there. He could have stopped
Mother simply by withholding the money, but he didn't.
Instead he trusted his Essie to keep me from harm and sent
half of his salary every week to supplement mine. "So you
can be sure to eat well," he said. Frank Brown didn't have
the foggiest notion of what the theatre was all about. He
couldn't be sustained, as Mother was, during our struggles
by dreams of glory. How he must have suffered. How mortifying it must have been for him having to explain away his
wife's hauling his eight-year-old off to New York.

I missed my father. I missed him terribly. And whenever
we could negotiate the fare we would, at my pleading, go
home to Washington for a Sunday. Graddy was housekeep-

ing for him and Father was hopefully keeping the home fires burning for his girls' permanent return.

Mother was convinced that this new world would release her from the shadows, but it didn't.

When freedom finally came to Essie Brown it was not so sweet. It came too late. During our first years in New York she was shy and frightened of the very people with whom she had once dreamed of mingling. Her vision of a perpetual soiree with those dazzling creatures from the world of light and laughter quickly vanished. Even then, people thought in labels. She was immediately identified as a "stage mother," and everyone knew that that meant she was a pushing, arrogant, battling pest. Those in the theatre who mattered resented her. There was something about me that aroused the paternal instinct in all of them. It went on for years— through Lew Fields, John Drew, William Gillette, George Tyler, and all those others who chipped in from the wings. Every single one of them resented "Stage Mother Brown." Each knew his influence was temporary and she would have the last word. After all, she was my mother! It outraged them to think that one so inadequate could have this power. If anyone of the many who hurt and humiliated her had taken the trouble to know her better, he would have been relaxed about my future in her hands. I'd like to think he'd have been a little humbled, too. Mother never resented them, outwardly—or fought back. It must have been hard, for she was Irish proud.

Mr. Fields, for example, rarely, if ever, spoke to her. He simply didn't see her at all. When he saw me he would break into that great warm smile of his, rush forward, pick me up, give me a hug, and ask what I'd been doing that day before I came to the theatre. Or he would tell me some story about his little daughter, Dorothy, who was almost my age. Then he'd release me to follow my mother, who by this time had drifted on out of his sight.

Later, when I played with John Drew, he would send his valet to my dressing room on high to escort me down for my nightly visit in the Empire star dressing room. Mother was never asked in there. It was the same with William Gillette in 1919 in *Dear Brutus*. When I eventually played the Empire as a star, I remember what fun we had making a big ceremony of Mother's entrance into that room. I remember, too, that she wondered if she should get a priest to exorcize "those two devils."

During those early days she obliterated herself and she endured. She was modest about her own capacity for helping me to grow as an actress, so she was delighted with every exposure to and every conversation I had with the illustrious, in the hope that I would pick up some crumb of knowledge. After the play at night, we would sit up in bed, munching our delicatessen sandwiches in our second-floor-back at Nathanson's rooming house, and going over each of those conversations, which I would have memorized. I was careful to do that, so Mother could sift the words like a prospector looking for nuggets. If an illuminating idea emerged, she would stash it away in her memory for future use. It always startled me to hear her, many years later, quoting some tip from Mr. Fields or Mr. Gillette that would help me solve the problem at hand.

Backstage encounters provided our only touch with people. My dressing-room mates were our only friends. They usually began the season furious at being saddled with us and ended by trying to adopt us. But there was no relaxing Mother's guard against loose-living characters who might have a bad influence on my future as an actress. I had to be kept pure. I had to be ready to ascend the throne in my true realm—

the legitimate theatre. As for the inhabitants of this lesser world, beloved friends though they were, I never saw them in their street clothes.

Mother, whose life had been crowded with family and friends at home, was a recluse in New York. Her pride and the prejudice of others rather narrowed our circle, and for a while we just had each other. We had a marvelous time. I had inherited Mother's rubber neck, and we prowled the streets and avenues of Little Old New York—the old ones at the tip of Manhattan and the new ones uptown. We devoured the colorful island whole, from the Aquarium at the Battery to Fort Belvedere up in Central Park—from below the ground on its nickel subway that could take you out to the seashore at Coney Island for sarsaparilla and hot dogs, and from the heights of the top deck of the Fifth Avenue bus that sailed along Riverside Drive to Grant's Tomb. Then there was the remarkable elevated train that passed people's windows like a magic carpet—so near that you could say hello to the fat mothers who leaned on the windowsills with babies, or the thin old men in bathrobes who sat staring at the world passing them by.

Opera matinees and trips to the museums of art and natural history and the shops—Vantine's for Mother and F.A.O. Schwarz for me—filled our days. And when we were tired, we rested in the fashionable hotels. Mother loved the lobbies of the old Waldorf, and the Plaza and the Astor.

We would screw up our courage, smooth our hair and dresses, and stroll into these gorgeous places, pretending to wait for someone who always, of course, stood us up. While we rested our weary feet, we would sit luxuriantly midst the potted palms and listen to both Victor Herbert's music played by a string ensemble and the exquisite clatter of tea cups and upper-crust conversation. We would gape at the elegantly dressed ladies leading their lives of silken leisure, until Mother was satisfied or self-consciously thought that our presence was arousing suspicion.

At this point, she would look at her watch with great ceremony. Then, with haughty impatience—outraged by our broken rendezvous—mother and daughter would rise from the brocade couch and depart in high dudgeon, thereby showing Mr. X a thing or two. Outside, we would explode with laughter and reward ourselves with a soda at nice Mr. Schrafft's, who had a small store near the theatre.

Mother invented a unique childhood for me and gave me delicious memories. Looking back, I wonder why I was so intent on moving my Mary to a small town for a "normal childhood." Perhaps because it was impossible for me to give over my whole life to her, as Brownie did with me.

Mother's natural ebullience made it difficult not to attract and respond to our dressing-room companions. And life got even better on the road.

The theatre with its swiftly changing scenes was the perfect background for Mother's restless spirit. She thrilled to the hectic, noisy life backstage and on tour. In the wings or an upper berth, a dingy hallroom or a freezing dressing room, Brownie belonged. She loved the whole frenetic existence and it suited her. She reveled in late rehearsals and train schedules, dinners of dry sandwiches tasting of wax and containers of never-hot-enough coffee.

Backstage was part of the theatre, and Mother had been bitten by the bug. She was always to have that sweet poison in her blood. With me on stage and herself behind it, Mother—despite everything—remained heartened.

❊   ❊   ❊

If I love actors it is because, one by one, from Lew Fields

to Ina Claire, they took me in hand, weighed my value, and —remarkably—found me worth their consideration. I would be nothing without them. I am their creation. I am their collaboration—based on an idea by my mother.

It wasn't immediately apparent that the beautiful world of make-believe I entered was—like all fairy tales—filled with the harshest realities. Making believe is easy for a child, and so my life in the theatre was one long birthday party. If I flourished at all it was the fault of others.

The first was Lew Fields. A shy, serious child had made this great comedian laugh. My simplicity, my brand-newness had attracted him. With his derby hat and oversized checked pants, his hayseed beard and wild eyes, Mr. Fields was a funny man and as good as Graddy Hayes and Brownie at making people laugh. His theatrical instincts told him that my grave little presence at his side would make them laugh louder.

It was Mr. Fields who first let me discover the gentle power that comes from creating laughter in a theatre. It is, for me, the sound of heaven.

Except for a time when the Gerry Society, a do-gooder organization, forbade my appearance in Chicago and a midget was hired to play my part, I happily worked with Mr. Fields in New York and on the road. Mother and I traveled all over the country, staying in any boarding houses or hotels that were within our means.

In those days, the theatre demanded of its members stamina, good digestion, the ability to adjust, and a strong sense of humor. There was no discomfort an actor didn't learn to endure. To survive, we had to be horses and we were.

With the death of "the road" and the birth of microphones, a working actor's life became easier; and with greater conveniences and protection, a lot of the necessary toughness disappeared along with the hardships. Certainly, I do not plead for exploitation and maltreatment of young actors, but stress of some sort will always be with us, and early buffeting helps build resistance to it.

I loved all the hard work. Except for missing Father, I couldn't have been happier.

Father seemed always to be waving goodbye at the railroad station, getting smaller and smaller in my life, his brave smile blurring more and more as we chugged away. Still, in my memory, it is he who was there to comfort me. It was he who—when I lay trembling with fright—stood stroking my hand as I went under gas during a tonsil operation. As I drifted into the unknown, I could feel the gentle stroke of my father's hand on mine and it was my only safety. I was not quite unconscious when the stroking stopped—no doubt at the doctor's suggestion—but when his hand was gone, I felt a moment of loss and pain I have never been able to forget. It was oddly my father's passivity and gentleness that eventually helped me through the many disillusionments and humiliations that are part of every public career.

At the age of eight, I was transported to a world of color and music, a world in which I always felt my blood tingle. I still missed my father. But I was a child, and was all over the place backstage, in every nook and cranny of this fairyland. The property man made me a little proscenium stage for my dressing-room table and the electricians cut miniature colored gelatins for me—ambers and blues and reds and greens—the colors of penny candy. What marvelous effects I would create in my own tiny theatre. I had no friends my own age and I didn't miss them. The other children in the show were "atmosphere" and when they weren't on, they played together in the alley, excluding me because I was a "principal." Already I was learning to live with the caste

system of the theatre. It prepared me for the sometime loneliness of stardom.

I was certainly never lonely backstage as a child. There
was too much going on. Ada Barclay, the wardrobe mistress,
was my idol. She sat all evening replacing spangles and
jewels and bows. Sitting there in her little room, surrounded
by scraps of brilliant color and rhinestones, swamped in
satins and veiling, she was a maker of magic. She should
have worn a crescented, cone-shaped hat with a wimple.

Miss Barclay allowed me to search the wings and stairs for
errant paillettes and bugle beads and sequins, which I
cached away in a flannel bag like rubies and emeralds. When
I collected enough, I would breathlessly lay them at her feet
like stardust, and her nimble fingers would return them to
those heavenly costumes.

Everyone was so kind to me—everyone but John Bunny.
The fat, kind, and jolly comedian soon to become one of the
Silent Screen's immortals was neither kind nor jolly, though
his fat was undeniable. He gluttonized, snorted, and slept
when he wasn't on stage, and he always had to be awakened
from one of his deep, noisy, ogre-like slumbers when it was
his cue. There were times when the stage manager would
pretend he had forgotten, so that I could rush to the rescue
by poking the grouchy giant awake, backing away in terror
but saving the day.

The King of this most wondrous domain was, of course,
the dear, gentle Lew Fields. I was his most devoted subject.

There was a bevy of kids in *Old Dutch*, and they gathered
like Lilliputians, first around the monumental Victor Herbert,
who wrote the music, and then around the homey Mr. Fields.
They scurried and crawled all over him at the instigation of
their ambitious mothers.

Brownie was always a snob in reverse. It was not cunning,
but her impeccable instinct and consideration, that prompted

her to insist that I do my job and keep my distance from the star. Piqued by my reserve, the brat-ridden comedian sought me out—making me, from that point onward, his very special ward. Straitlaced and old-worldly, he was the conscience of the wayward company and the discreet hands over my ears.

He was always docking actors and stagehands for using questionable language near me. Charlie was also this protective later on. It has been one of the maddening ironies of my life that, from the beginning, I have always been attracted to rogues and rascals and inevitably they turn respectable in my presence.

Of course, I was a baby then, but I didn't need protection. I was completely insulated by my own purity. I was surrounded by the most glorious sinners and loved them all. Better than any acting school was the experience I had meeting such a grab bag of characters early in life. I have always belonged to what I call the subway school of acting—that moving, roaring classroom where one studies fellow passengers. Mother and I used to play "Who are they and where are they going?," although I stared so intently that she would have to elbow me back to reality.

Meeting and getting to know my fellow actresses was even better. One of my favorites was Billie Coupier, one of the showgirls in *Old Dutch*. We dressed together, and I thought she was the most beautiful creature in the whole world. I was not alone in this judgment, because Billie had a limousine and beautiful furs, a magnificent apartment, and a line of top-hatted, Inverness-caped gentlemen friends.

Virtually every girl in these shows had a "protector"—a man of station and elegance who sent her strings of pearls and marquisite buckles and diamond broaches, as well as the nightly long-stemmed American beauties.

It was an accepted convention of the day, and there was

style and grace to these brief romances. I suppose the quality of the notable men set the tone. These socialites were above censure. Whatever the reason, they made it possible for 35-dollar-a-week chorus girls to live like princesses.

These gentlemen certainly knew how to admire young ladies. They had perfected it to a fine art. What a pity the amateurs have taken over!

How elegant it all used to be. I just skipped and sashayed my happy way midst these mauve proceedings, so innocent that I could actually have witnessed the wildest of Bacchanals and believed it to be the latest production number in the *Follies*.

The stage-door Johnnies would wait patiently in the alley and then carry my friends off in hansom cabs to what I believed was a great ballroom with crystal chandeliers and lots of potted palms, where wine would be drunk from their slippers, their hands kissed constantly and where everyone would then dance till dawn. How I envied those happy, beautiful girls.

Billie Coupier looked like a bon-bon, pink and white and creamy. She belonged in a little gold wrapping placed in a paper lace cup—the very best in a box of Louis Sherry confections. Fulsome, with crinkling eyes, she was always laughing—and why not?

After the show I would watch her dress and stare wide-eyed at her aigrettes and chiffons, her jewels and rice-powdered back. She was always off to Delmonico's or Rector's; sometimes on rainy days she would have a champagne cup and chicken à la king sent in from Shanley's across the street and share it with us. The champagne cup was filled with sticks of fresh pineapple and orange slices and—best of all—had a maraschino cherry. These would be mine. And there was just a hint of the champagne tingle. For years, success meant simply that I could have champagne and chicken à la king three times a day. It was the panache of fame and fortune, and I dreamed that someday this would be my fare.

I kept this dream all through the years between plays, when Mother and I would share a single 50¢ meal in an Italian restaurant. She would get the savory antipasto, I the hot nourishing minestrone. Mother would then try negotiating the spaghetti around her fork while I devoured the chicken and spinach. The sharp salad was Brownie's, the tricolored spumoni mine. Even the wine was divided. Mother would dye my glass of water red with a tablespoon of chianti and add a cube of sugar to sweeten it. It was simply awful but wonderfully festive and grown-up. We would click glasses and toast the future, pretending it was Billie Coupier's Piper Heidsieck Brut!

4

In *Old Dutch*, I found my Prince Charming and fell in love for the first time. He was tall and he was skinny and he wore a green suit. He looked just like a string bean. His name was Vernon Castle, and he became the center of my life. He took me to his tender heart. The iron stairs backstage were too steep for me to climb quickly enough and at each performance, after my scene with Mr. Fields, he would sweep me up and carry me to my dressing room. I would wait breathlessly for the moment. He became my reason for being, and his funny little mash-notes and jokes and gifts were like draughts of life-giving oxygen. I ate, drank, and talked nothing but Vernon Castle. Poor Mother. I drove her mad with my adoration of him.

Vernon was a delight. He knew how to enter into a child's world and, better still, how to make a child feel grown-up.

His games were enchanting, our mock romance fraught with drama. He would have his dresser hand me a note as I walked offstage and I would rush to the privacy of my dressing room to read it. The note would speak of his extreme jealousy or wretchedness due to some fabricated attention I had paid to old Mr. Fields or the porcine John Bunny. He would sometimes, in the conceit, be my husband, or sometimes an ardent suitor. The notes would be answered by me as quickly as I could think up clever replies. Vernon was playing a game. I was not. I was the string bean's adoring dream-wife.

My world was rocked one day when I heard that Billie Coupier was leaving the show for some glamorous, amorous reason. It was shattered when I heard that it was a sweetheart of Vernon's who would replace her and share my dressing room. A sweetheart!

I hid in the shadows the day Vernon proudly strolled in and introduced the slim, beautiful girl to everybody. "Where's Helen?" Vernon asked as I retreated further into the dark corner. I wished a trap door would open under her.

She's a bean pole, I decided viciously—conveniently ignoring the fact that they were obviously made for each other. *And that ugly name!*

Irene Foote was a socialite from New Rochelle. She was a horsewoman, a swell, and very stylish, so Brownie informed me. But I saw a nervous, skinny non-professional who had never appeared on stage before. She got Billie's part despite all my reservations; and you couldn't hear her dialogue three feet away. She followed Vernon around like a puppy, unsure of herself, tripping over ropes, bumping into flats, under everyone's feet. It was doubly painful to me. It was absolute betrayal! My Vernon had fallen in love with an amateur!

She had no theatrical ambitions whatever, but Vernon was determined to make her his partner. She was so disinterested

that she would shrug her shoulders when told that she
couldn't be heard, or that her back was to the audience. It
was all a lark to Miss Amateur Irene Foote.

I couldn't have been meaner. When Irene walked into that
dressing room the first time and asked what she should do
about makeup, I quickly answered, "Ask Willis B. Sweatnam
what he uses!" Mr. Sweatnam was a famous black-face comedian in the show. She bought a box of minstrel's makeup. I
don't know what I expected to happen; but I was foiled.
Vernon found her naiveté touching, and I just made him love
her more than ever with my mischief!

When we went on tour, my contempt for this creature
knew no bounds. My swain was far too busy with reality to
keep up our game; and though he remained a loving friend,
I wasn't so young that I didn't know that not only Billie
Coupier had been replaced.

Irene's presence made me work harder than ever to be
good for Vernon. When Lew Fields, as part of our routine,
shocked at something or other, stretched his legs and I slid
off his lap to the floor, I made the trip down funnier than
ever. The audience roared but my jealous little heart was
breaking.

I hated and scorned Irene's every attempt to sing or dance
or speak her lines. I laughed at her and Irene joined me. She
actually laughed at herself and I looked very darkly on such
sans souci. She could not take herself or her work seriously,
but I had to. She now was a permanent member of our
company.

In *Summer Widowers,* I played Psyche Finnegan, an
early-day Lucy from *Peanuts.* I worked with a tiny man
named Will Archer who was dressed as a little boy in a
bumfreezer and Eton collar. Will would stand intently con-
templating a beautiful raspberry tart that made my mouth
water. "Look what I got for going on an errand," Will would

say proudly, "a raspberry tart!" About to dig his teeth into the sweet, he was stopped by my subtle observation,

"That's not raspberry. Anyone can see it's strawberry."

"No, it's not! Take a bite and see," the poor ninny would say.

Little Psyche would try a bite. "I don't *know*, Billy, I think it's *black*berry. No. No! Let me try again. Maybe it's *goose*berry! No, no . . ."

Of course, it was Psyche who devoured the whole tart in her fraudulent quest for truth—and not the little boy who had earned it.

The scene was funny, and one night, probably thinking of my hatred of Irene, by this time married to Vernon, I added insult to injury by wiping my hands on Will Archer's sleeve after finishing his tart. I had been directed to brush my hands of any crumbs, but this was the final indignity, and when I walked offstage, the gesture made even funnier his line, "You can't never trust a woman." Both Will and later Mr. Fields asked me to keep the business in. The laugh was far bigger; and I felt truly superior to Irene, whom I considered the *second* Mrs. Castle. I remained jealous and contemptuous of her until one afternoon on tour.

I think we were at the Riviera Theatre at 96th and Broadway after 14 weeks in Atlantic City and points south. Vernon had asked Mr. Fields if he would audition him and Irene as dancers. Over the summer they had worked up a routine and hoped that, for the next show, the star would allow them to share a spot. Mr. Fields adored Vernon almost as much as I did, but for some unknown reason he kept refusing to see their act. He repeatedly postponed the audition but, at last, he relented between two shows on a Saturday.

A small naked bulb hung on stage and the rest of the theatre was in Stygian darkness when Mr. Fields felt his way down the aisle and said,

"So—go ahead, Vernon."

"Can't we have some light?" Vernon asked.

"Go ahead, Vernon. I'm waiting." It was obvious that Mr. Fields was going to make it tough.

"But you won't be able to see what I've worked out!"

"I came—I'm seeing."

Something happened to me as I stood in the wings watching them silhouetted against the glaring bulb. Those two string beans were beautiful. It was so unfair. With my outrage at the injustice, my jealousy vanished. *Please give them light,* I found myself praying. *Please give them a chance. . . .*

Vernon and Irene had no choice but to do their routine in the shadows. They were barely finished with their first number when Mr. Fields stood up, said that he'd seen enough, and then felt his way back up the aisles and out of the theatre. Whatever his reasons, his heart was dead set against their joint ambitions. Mine just melted.

"He'll be sorry," I heard Irene say most distinctly. Anger had given her volume, clarity, and obvious purpose. A scant three years later, my Vernon and his lovely wife were the famous Castles, a sensation on both sides of the Atlantic. They used to call such stars the toast of two continents, and they certainly were.

When Vernon sent us tickets and Mother and I went backstage to see them after their performance, it was the first time I ever saw such a dressing room. The draperies, the chaise lounge, her dogs—and she had a secretary! The whole entourage impressed me out of my senses. Everything about Irene was chic. Vernon certainly knew what he was doing when he chose her. His eye was keener than Mr. Fields's and less jaundiced than mine. My first dream of love!

It took two New York seasons and as many road tours to relax Mother's strict rules against consorting outside the theatre with the questionable characters of the musical comedy world. Then she went all the way in her blessed, inconsistent fashion and took in to live with us a real fallen angel, if ever there was one. Her name was Pat Neaves. She was a snub-nosed, enchanting colleen—Dublin Irish and absolutely adorable. Because she was a "medium," she could share a dressing room with a principal player. "Mediums" did a bit of dancing and usually handled some dialogue. Showgirls just showed off their beauty; and "ponies" danced and kicked a lot.

Pat actually did a number with three other girls. Dressed in grey chiffon tipped with pink, with pink ruffles and demure sunkist-maiden bonnets, they sang a risqué little song while they twitched their skirts well above their ankles. It went like this:

> Just a glimpse of lingerie
> Is attractive in a most attractive way (*twitch*)
> Just a bit of frou frou
> Tied with silken bows
> Discreetly will expose (*twitch*)
> A glimpse of silken hose (*twitch*)
> Just a slight suggestion of your charms
> To best advantage you'll display
> Though in other ways
> You try the gaze
> Of any fellow's eyes
> You'll get his mortgage with a glimpse of lingerie.

With this last line, the twitching became convulsive as they brought down the house.

I was utterly enslaved by Pat when in dead seriousness she asked me to watch a performance and tell her if she was all right. Heavy with the responsibility, I took to watching her religiously, and could quite honestly report nightly what she wanted to hear: that she made the rest of the quartet pale by comparison.

Pat was a darlin' girl, all right, and loyal to her huge family back in Ireland. There was a crew of them—all but one younger than Pat. She sent home every cent she could spare, which explained her readiness to sponge dinners and "borrow" makeup, habitually. She'd read us the family letters in our dressing room and always she would end up teary-eyed and laughing at the same time. Her downfall in the company that sent her hurtling into our lives came about in this way.

George Monroe, the star of our show, was a portly comic, an uninhibited slapstick artist who always appeared as a very grand lady with a huge fan—the better to whack everybody on the head with. Like Beatrice Lillie, he was that perfect mixture of elegance and roughhouse that makes for great comedy. I used to love to watch him perform, but I kept out of his way in the wings. Offstage he was gross, grumpy, and gruff—a horrid man. As soon as the show left for the tour, like a pasha of old, our star looked over the harem and selected Pat to keep him amused for the duration. Since it meant bigger checks to send home, she accepted with alacrity and moved into his suite at the best hotel.

Word shot back to Mr. Fields's office in New York from our company manager and a sharp reprimand was wired back to Monroe for conduct beneath the standards of a Lew Fields production. Pat was to be fired. That was the first time I ever saw my mother speak up. She begged, she argued, even threatened to remove me from such an uncharitable atmosphere. It was particularly funny because Mr. Fields was being that strict about company deportment mainly to protect me! Well, Mother ended by taking Pat in to live with us, and it was a happy solution. It insured Pat's continued help to her family—and increased mine by one. Pat was the first of many roommates, and her tales of the London theatre were my bedtime stories. Mother was especially taken with her anecdotes of chorus girls who had married earls, but I loved to hear about Pat when she was a child actress, like me—only so different! From the age of nine she had been earning her way all on her own—without a mother to take care of her. It awed me. First she managed to get jobs in crowd scenes in the local Dublin theatres simply by hanging around the stage doors and making a pest of herself, and then, beating her way to London somehow, she started landing parts in the Christmas Pantomime.

In *Babes in the Wood* she was "Kind Robin," who covered the lost sleeping Babes with leaves to keep them warm in the damp forest .This solicitous business was the second-act curtain, and Pat confessed without shame that she padded her first and only solo scene so outrageously—hopping about, ignoring the frantic voices from backstage, flapping her wings, tossing leaves in the air, and shaking her tail in a kind of travesty of Swan Lake—that even the sleeping Babes themselves were angrily hissing, "Get on with it!"

After this opening night self-indulgence, the program might have read "Baby Pat Neaves as Kind Robin," but backstage she would never have been recognized by such a description. "Damned Robin" was more like it.

"Tell that *damned* Robin she'll get her pay, but she can't wriggle in front of everyone else or I'll smack her!"

"If that *damned* Robin doesn't stop poking about in my makeup kit . . ."

"Where's that *damned* Robin? It's time for her entrance."

Pat ended the recital of her dubious doings with resignation. "What are you going to do?" she asked with a sigh. "People are *so* harsh."

She was an education to Mother. Once the plunge had been taken and we survived this hazardous exposure to other members of the troupe, Mother went all out. Pat's fundamental wholesomeness convinced her that people's morals were their own business. Brownie was no longer concerned with morals, but with manners. Her candor and authenticity now attracted all who were genuine and fun. Only the vulgar, the rude, and the pretentious disturbed Mother. These were now the vices against which she guarded me.

Pat Neaves was the first of a long line of girls that Mother took in with us. Though the rest of my roommates were pure and absolutely above reproach, I remember them fondly anyway. Some, especially Jean Dixon, gratefully. Certainly, none of them could have been more discreet or delicious than our darlin' Pat.

For all those years before my marriage, I always had a "sister," and Mother had another daughter. I don't pretend to understand her compulsion to adopt other young aspiring actresses, but it would seem probable that she identified with the whole string of them, each time reliving her own tortuous struggle to establish an identity—always without success. That kind of frustration can shrivel a heart or stretch it. My mother's stretched.

Pat was eventually replaced by the Hess Sisters, with whom Mother and I shared two rooms: two double beds and a single bath between. Rea and Hannah were hard-working, easygoing girls who were "Russian" dancers in one of the musicals I appeared in. They had long dark hair and Cossack costumes and a mama to whom they sent their pay checks.

Every morning Rea and Hannah, still in pajamas, their long braids bouncing, would hold onto the foot of the bed and squat, extending first one leg and then the other. I always joined them in order to keep in shape.

They used to compete with me after the show to see who could eat more blueberry pie; they took me to the zoo and helped me with my lessons, which were sent in by the Professional Children's School; and they taught me the Russian *kazatsky*. When we were invited by their Orthodox mother to a seder in the Bronx, the food and ceremony were so impressive that I seriously considered becoming Jewish.

* * *

We were barely settling into the routine of the theatre when Fred Thompson, who had directed me with the Columbia Players in Washington, urged Mother to let me play in one of the movies being made at the Vitagraph Studio, where he was now directing.

It was considered undignified for an actor to work in this medium unless he was starving, so Mother quite literally sneaked me out to Vitagraph, where we bumped smack into mean old John Bunny. We were first stunned and then amused.

"I won't tell on you," Mr. Bunny blustered, "if you won't tell on me!"

And the pact was kept. Mother did everything to disguise me—curling my hair for the first time and changing my mouth with makeup. But when my first picture in support of a collie dog named Jean was shown, there I was, unmistakably me, but me looking very odd indeed. The silver screen was hardly the place to hide.

Jean and The Calico Doll was the name of the epic. Maurice Costello was also in it. The plot was simple. I fell down a ravine in my pastel travels. Jean, the faithful collie, in order to save my life, grabbed my doll and raced back to my father, who followed his hairy guide to the scene of the accident. We traveled to Fort Lee, New Jersey, on the ferry to make that classic. The stars, Florence Turner and Maurice Costello, joined everyone else, including camera and propmen, and sat on those long slatted benches drinking hot coffee at dawn. Nobody was very fancy in those days.

Making pictures was a lark and the most vagabond existence. We'd all get into a long line of automobiles with tripods, cameras, props, and lunches. Then we'd drive until we saw a lovely estate that might serve as a setting for the company. If the house and surrounding land seemed right, an official hand would wave the caravan to stop and out we'd jump, to steal the view as a background to our plot.

We would hurriedly play a scene on the velvety lawn and in and out of the sycamore trees and hydrangea bushes, and then run before a window was opened and a threatening voice would send us packing. We always ran faster than the owners or their servants, who sometimes came out to chase us off their property. The audacity of us—it was marvelous!

I had much more fun in those tuppenny thrillers than I ever did at MGM 25 years later. All the spontaneity was gone by then. Everything had become slick and self-conscious. Everyone was important, and innocence was lost.

In another one of these early quickies, I was saved from a fire. While I was being rescued and carried down a ladder by a real fireman, pretending that I was petrified, Brownie watched from across the street, where a crowd of spectators had gathered. One of them—a large, hatchet-faced woman— nudged Brownie with her elbow.

"The mother of that poor little child should be arrested," she announced loudly.

She was a born leader, this woman, and her suggestion started the rest of the mob grumbling. Just before the movie scene was completed, my guilt-ridden darling fled for fear of detection. If I had run to her, crying, "How was that, Mother?" she would have been tarred and feathered.

*   *   *

Mother continued to chart my course and keep things shipshape as we sailed along—leaving Father in our wake.

Though others more qualified periodically took over my career, Mother's influence was more constant and more lasting. Certainly, I resented bitterly what I believed to be her over-criticism, but that's because I suspected she was right. Mother yearned for excellence and the only passing mark in her book was A.

She only concerned herself with my performance and could be curiously unaggressive with theatre people.

"Let the lighting men light you; let the director direct. Stick to your acting!"

Mother always warned me never to argue about billing. "It's the public that makes stars, Helen." She could have added, "It's the public that keeps them stars."

I sometimes think that, despite everything else, what matters most with parents is taste. It goes deep, as do the choices that determine it. Mother's eye caught everything. It was she who first noticed my many mannerisms, the dreadful habit of touching my face as if to make sure it was still there, my tendency to hunch my shoulders when I was nervous. All of this was symptomatic of the same thing—fear. I was trying to hide from the audience. My shyness was taking its toll on stage.

Mother's constant protection, I fear, was weakening me. It kept me from developing initiative and confidence. I wonder, looking back, how different things might have been had I been allowed to grow on my own. I'll never know. I was Mother's creation, and offstage I was so timid that when I spied Maude Adams coming toward us one day on 40th Street, near the Empire Theater, I flew across the street, almost getting killed by a frightened horse.

When Brownie asked me what in God's name I had done, I answered, "But it was Maude Adams. I thought I might get in her way or something."

*   *   *

Mother and I were back in Washington on Father's door-

step when the Fields's musicals were *fini*. I was 12 then—
what was called in the theatre "the awkward age"—and there
were no roles being offered me. Father couldn't have been
happier. Hoping it would be permanent, that our adventure
was over, he bought a little house for us on 18th Street near
Rock Creek Park and the zoo. Listening to the Victrola on
our front porch on a summer evening, the roar of lions was
a strange accompaniment to the voices of Mary Garden and
Beniamino Gigli. But the primitive undercurrent was wildly
prophetic.

Though I was cozy and content to be home with Father,
Mother was again a seething captive. That taste of freedom
had whetted her appetite. She would now crave it as never
before, and forever be in despair without it.

Circumstances made it impossible to cart me off again
simply to look for work. Knowing only the Fields's office and
still smarting from familiar rebuffs from the help, as well as
the employers, the unknown was too terrifying for her even
to contemplate. Mother's drive was, unfortunately, never
accompanied by authority. That was why she was never to
be more than a success once removed.

Then, too, she knew only too well my devotion to Father
and couldn't separate us without a definite reason—a firm
commitment in New York. Mother was now trapped as never
before, as caged as those lions, and like them she was filled
with rebellion and despair. To her credit, she tried to accept
her lot: putting up preserves, collecting recipes, cleaning
house, and hating every solitary moment of it. She was acting out a role for which she was totally unsuited. She who
had been born with an unerring eye for truth in performance cringed at her own lack of authenticity.

The strain must have been agony. Her incredible energy,
unchanneled, ran wild. Joining a bridge club, seeing old and
new friends, she fled the house more and more in the eve-

nings. Her natural gaiety turned to giddiness. A line I was to say in *Dear Brutus* best describes her:

"To be very gay, my dearest dear, is so near to being very sad."

Mother's gaiety was constant and hollow, like the rosy flush of health that comes with a fever. Then it became obvious that, always committed to a fantasy world, she had found the quickest path to it.

She knew her way instinctively: it was in her blood. The Hayes family curse now threatened her. Like her father and her sister Mamie and her brother Tom, like countless other wayward Irish, Mother began to drink.

Our little house came tumbling down as Mother alternated between light-headed evenings and guilt-ridden daily retreats. Some nights I would hear my father's anguished voice in the hall as he helped her to their bedroom: "Oh, Essie! Essie!"

Children are not burdened with tolerance. Filled with horror and shame, I would bury my face in the pillow and I would cry.

True to the way of our class, with its narrow code, we made a dark and guilty secret of her problem. It was as if she were given to spells of madness. How my shame must have hurt her. On the days of her self-reproach and moody withdrawal I cooked the dinners for Father and Mother as well, between school and my studies. We had lost Graddy by this time, and there was no one to steady our little household. I wish I could report that I understood and sympathized. I didn't. At the time, I minded our reversal of roles and hated her for making Father unhappy. I had discovered, for the first time, that one could love and hate in concert.

I see now how even Mother's demons helped shape me. They were hardly joyous companions for a small child, but **her weakness made me** strong. As the years passed, her problem grew. It was her hell. It was my crucible. I was taught to accept responsibility—to be leaned on, and not clinging. I was taught by my mother's demons to stand alone.

I had no idea that it was my mother who was actually the weaker of my parents. Her defenses had fooled me, and my sympathies lay with my gentle father. Mother was always exploding at home, and nothing except the World Series could make Father raise his voice. He would simply say, "In a hundred years, no one will know the difference." His acceptance would enrage Mother more than battle.

One day I came home from school and walked into their bedroom. There was a bay window and the sun was flooding the room. Daddy was standing, profile in silhouette, a haze around him. Specks of dust hung suspended in the shaft of light behind his head. His hands were together, church-steeple style.

"Daddy," I shouted, as I rushed toward him. Then I saw the tears rolling down his face. There wasn't the slightest doubt who had put them there.

I heard Mother at the icebox and I ran down the hall into the kitchen—my anger almost transporting me. I grabbed her by her arms and shook her. It was the first and last time in my life I ever dared do such a thing and, looking back with understanding, it is even more painful now. I actually shook my mother, hissing, "Go inside and say you're sorry, do you hear? Say you're sorry to my father!"

We were both so frightened that we just stood staring at each other. My heart was pounding, but I didn't move. Mother's shoulders fell and she did what I asked.

The die was cast, and the reversal of our roles was now complete. We never spoke of it, but we both knew.

*　　*　　*

It is fascinating seeing it all from such a distance, through the wrong end of the opera glass. Mother was a child and more and more came to depend on me. I had felt it, oddly, always, even when I was very small. Still, she had her sovereignty and her incredible reach for excellence. She yearned for quality and set her sights on perfection. It was contagious, this fever, and I caught it.

It was the greatest good fortune that, at just this time, Charles Frohman sent for me. God knows what would have happened, and how we would have ended, if he had not.

Jessie Glendening, who had been Dearest to my Little Lord Fauntleroy, had recommended me for a part in *The Prodigal Husband,* starring John Drew. He was looking for a ten-year-old who resembled Miss Glendening sufficiently to play her as a child in the first act. Because of my size, I could pass for that age, although I was now 13. Also, when Miss Glendening and I had played together, everyone had remarked on our likeness and our identical ash-blonde hair.

Mr. Drew, it seemed, was ready to strangle the next frizzed-blonde child who auditioned for him. Actors work and slave—and it is the color of your hair that can determine your fate in the end.

It is true that Miss Glendening, when she advised Charles Frohman and John Drew to send for me, told them that she had seen "a light shining within the child." Mother saw a light at the end of the tunnel and she regained her balance immediately. We were entering the world of John Drew and Charles Frohman and the Empire Theater. With the air of a queen mother delivering the princess royal to her rightful domain, Mother stepped aboard the Congressional Limited bound for New York.

*   *   *

It is difficult to describe the impact of John Drew's celebrity. There are no stars today who can approximate this man's magnitude. He was the supreme elegant, the taste-maker of his day.

When he first looked down at me over his great nose, his chin almost matching the beak in its thrust, his black moustache separating the two aggressive features like a referee at one of his beloved prizefights, I was saved from terror only by the twinkle in one of his grey eyes. The other one was slightly cocked. As evidence of the gentleman's style and authority in such matters, he absolutely made a virtue of this asymmetry, carrying it off with such dash that other men in his presence looked pedestrian without it.

Mr. Drew's face could only have belonged to an actor of his time. No senator, general, or emperor would have dared to look so classically pre-arranged. He was larger than life— a Victorian overstatement like the Albert Memorial.

He was always dressed either in white tie and tails or a shooting jacket, since, onstage or off, his life was composed of a series of stylish vignettes. Drawing rooms, conservatories, and hunting preserves were his *mise-en-scène,* and I honestly don't believe he ever did the things that make the rest of us mortals. He was certainly the most beloved and idolized actor of his time.

Thanks to Mr. Drew, my transition from musical comedy to drama was peak-hopping. I went from the best of one field to the best of the other. Mr. Frohman had under his aegis Maude Adams, Billie Burke, William Gillette, and Ethel Barrymore, as well as her redoubtable uncle, John Drew.

The Empire Theater was the heart of the American stage. C. F., as Mr. Frohman was called, orchestrated the season like a great conductor. He would open a play at the Empire starring Mr. Drew and then send it on tour, while Maude Adams played the second part of the season. Ethel Barrymore would then open a play while Miss Adams went on the road. Miss Barrymore would then take her play out, while Miss Burke opened in New York. The sun never seemed to set on this empire.

Not only the constellation of stars, but the productions as well, had an unmistakable tone. This was the era of lady and gentleman actors, who vied with the stylish audience, which, in turn, emulated them. I was being launched legitimately under the very best auspices—in one of the season's worst plays.

The Prodigal Husband was a sleazy romantic comedy which someone bothered to translate from the French. Playing a *boulevardier* who adopts tiny Simone on the convenient death of her mother, his *concierge,* the star not only lands on the floor playing with the child but, one act and a few years later, falls in love with her. Captured and purified by the innocence of Simone, now played by Miss Glendening, the gentleman gives up his life of pleasure to settle down and marry her. The scenes were saccharine and uncharacteristic of John Drew.

The *haute monde* converged on 39th and Broadway to witness John Drew getting his fingers sticky in this trifle. Not since Diamond Jim Brady and Lillian Russell knocked everybody's eyes out from their sparkling box at the *Old Dutch* premiere had Mother and I ever seen anything like the audience at our opening at the Empire. The gilded *bijou* of a theatre was glittering with jewels.

All society was there, and Mother was in seventh heaven. On dazzling display out front—waiting for Mr. Drew and, willy-nilly, me—were all of Brownie's idols, dressed to the teeth in their fine feathers, pearls, furs, and blinding diamonds. Long, white-gloved arms politely waved to each other until the whole orchestra looked like a sea of swans.

As a matter of fact, peeking through the curtain that successful night on the eve of World War I, I didn't know I was watching an epoch die. Life was never to be quite the same again for anyone—least of all, me.

Mr. Drew and Mr. Frohman had a rare relationship. As producer and star, they had a mutual respect and affection that transcended all differences. *Prodigal Husband* was not a hit and John Drew had known it wouldn't be. He had resisted appearing in it and was proven right. Nevertheless, it didn't stop him from taking the play on a five-month tour that could make up the financial loss the Empire engagement incurred. It was felt that the small towns would sell out simply on his great name. This was an act of pure devotion on John Drew's part.

The men were true friends, and a less likely pair there never was—the handsome, dashing patrician and the little, round, slant-eyed Buddha. Mr. Frohman was so gentle— their association such a tranquil one.

I saw Mr. Drew angry with Mr. Frohman only once, from a great distance and with good reason. The producer cabled that he was returning from a European business trip.

"Stay there," John Drew wired back. "Don't come back now. It's dangerous."

"I'm on my way on the next boat," Charles Frohman answered.

The star was ablaze with anger. "If the Huns sink you, I'll never forgive you," he cabled Mr. Frohman.

The Germans torpedoed the *Lusitania,* and our good friend was drowned. There are no words to describe John Drew's shock. His flippant wire would haunt him forever. He never jousted with the fates again. He reserved his wit for the answerable.

The newspapers were filled with details of the sinking, and

Charles Frohman was all over the front pages. The whole audience was aware of the tragedy; Mr. Frohman's theatre was suddenly a mausoleum.

It was quite an experience playing that night. Mr. Drew had lost his friend and I had lost Mr. Drew. He was nowhere on that stage that evening. He was simply a series of reflexes. I played my scenes with a tailor's dummy.

The whole theatre mourned Charles Frohman; the grief-stricken Maude Adams went into retirement on his death.

Rumors flew for years afterward that Mr. Frohman was my father. Some genius created the story that Maude Adams was my mother and her lover, C. F., my natural father. Where that left Brownie and Father was a mystery.

No one knows where these canards get their start. I only know they are hard to finish off. Mother actually heard one knowledgeable theatre buff informing an all-too-willing listener all about it one day, as she stood looking at one of the glass-enclosed photographs of me outside the Empire Theater many years later.

"That's right, Carrie. She's the love-child of Maude Adams and Daniel Frohman," the woman said, mixing brothers as well as parents.

Her mis-information was endless, but the woman's tone was one which forbade contradiction.

Mother was about to tell the woman off, as only she could. In fact, she was looking forward to it. But she suddenly caught a glimpse of herself reflected in the glass. It was a wet day and Brownie was picking me up backstage after doing some errands. She looked a sight, she thought. My career always came first.

"I know it sounds silly, Dear, but suddenly it was far better that those fools think Maude Adams is your mother, than Biddy Bedelia. And that's exactly who I look like today in this getup!"

5

LEGENDS die hard. They survive as truth rarely does. Someone once said that history is a chronological list of lies. My Charlie used to find the truth unchallenging and quite candidly created the most amazing tales to displace it. He was a writer and far too imaginative to settle for the simple facts. Our daughter, Mary, as a 15-year-old once explained the loss of her suitcase with a tale of a gamine, who, at the railway station, asked her some directions. As Mary answered, the little girl suddenly opened a box and threw cocoa in Mary's face, blinding her as she made off with the valise. Cocoa was the weapon used in this strange robbery. The imagination!

This mad tale has outlived many truths and, peculiarly enough, offers a glimpse of the fey, Charlie-like quality Mary had. There was a giggle in her soul, and she never could take anything too seriously. I suppose my concern about the bag was out of hand, and she simply had to embroider a tale to finish the whole business. Of course, it was possible. The truth is difficult to fathom sometimes.

Our son, Jim, small enough to be Jamie, had a terrible feud with our French poodle, Turvey. The little boy, so beautiful and sweet, was an absolute horror with this dog, and we caught him time and time again as he hit the dumb brute. Jamie was very young, not yet able to talk, but I was convinced that there was some imp in him that had to be exorcised, some trait we had to destroy before he grew to be a monster.

If we had not been camera bugs and caught the fleeting truth on film, we never would have discovered the real villain. Every time little Jamie started to put a cookie in his mouth, Turvey would steal it. That dog was so sly and so quick that all the naked eye ever caught was the effect and not the cause. Poor victimized Jamie. We thought for a while we had a bully for a son. Instead, we had a furry thief in the house. It is the effect that is lasting, the final image that clings to the retina like the bright after-glare of a naked bulb.

The Parthenon was built ever so slightly askew, so that from a distance it would look geometrically perfect. What, then, is the truth? I've come to think that in life, as in art, the revelation of truth frequently depends upon artifice.

Nowadays, in the theatre, artifice is scorned as a bag of tricks. I have been accused of using tricks for so long that I feel like Merlin. Well, if for one single moment I have created some magic, then I plead guilty. I certainly served an apprenticeship with some real sorcerers.

*   *   *

John Drew might have been Broadway's greatest star, but he was not a great actor. Truth had nothing to do with his approach to a part. As a matter of fact, he was the greatest of the cardboard players—handsomely tailored and beautifully mannered. Someone once said that Mr. Drew didn't act on stage: he behaved.

Each role was an extension of himself and I'm sure that, were he to have played Genghis Khan, that brute would have emerged an Edwardian lion. Still, Mr. Drew was a magician: when he was on stage, you could look at no one else. Presence cannot be learned, but one certainly recognizes the authority that comes with it and notes the dwarfing of those surrounding actors who lack it.

Just a couple of seasons ago, while playing in Pirandello's *Right You Are, If You Think You Are,* I was witness to a phenomenal example of this power.

At every performance, Signora Ponza, a minor but pivotal character, walked on stage and stood, a woman swathed and hidden under widow's weeds, an enigma in deep mourning. Utterly unidentifiable, she stood as the plot whirled round her. After a few words, she was gone. This had been played alternately by several of the repertory company's excellent young actresses. One night, I was surprised at the round of applause following her exit, since it was the first time that had ever happened. The mystery was solved when I discovered that at the last moment, on an impulse, Rosemary Harris had stepped into the costume to play the part.

Not a single bit of business was changed. But at that one performance the mass of black veils was a pillar of smoke; it had become a shadow of tragedy. It is remarkable that the actress's will and energy can so quickly capture an audience. That is the meaning of stardom. It was all projection of Self —most gratifying to the public, who ate it up.

Mr. Drew achieved this through personal magnetism and strength of will. I marvelled at his enormous self-discipline. A great drinker, Mr. Drew never touched the bottle until after the performance was over. The quart of Haig and

Haig awaited his late supper. This was a rule proved by one exception.

It was an Ash Wednesday matinee, when his eyes—never in agreement—suddenly locked in mortal combat. Both his eyes were now cocked. He had toasted the arrival of Lent and this long, long drink was the last for 40 days. That's discipline. He could easily have given up Harvard beets, as so many devout drinkers do. Even at that matinee, only his eyes revealed his state; he never once lost his poise.

One Sunday, in a one-horse town on the *Prodigal Husband* tour, a group of us tried in vain to find a place to eat. The townsfolk took the Sabbath seriously and eating out was obviously a brand-new sin. We homeless actors were starving. At last, a man directed us to a rickety lunch-wagon near the railroad tracks.

Ravenous, we wove our way dramatically to the oasis with the mock desperation of starvelings. Arriving at the diner, we relaxed into wild laughter that made everyone at the counter turn. There, sitting on a stool with a local blonde and packing away a steak and country-fried potatoes, was our elegant Mr. Drew. His presence transformed the wagon into Delmonico's. He rose, and, with the flourishing gesture of d'Artagnan entertaining all the queens of France, offered us the stools next to him.

"I am so pleased, my dears, that you were able to attend." What élan! No one has ever thrown away a line as he did.

* * *

A tour with John Drew was filled with bouquets of violets and no plumbing, with French lessons and a search for shelter. The extremes were typical. Aboard the train that would take us from town to town, I would go every afternoon to the gentleman's drawing room to study the French lessons the nuns so relentlessly kept sending. He not only worked with me, but read aloud from a beautifully illustrated edition of *Jeanne d'Arc* which he eventually gave me. Still, there were two things this man could not teach me: how to act and how to speak French properly. The sisters back in Washington all sounded like Clemenceau compared to this lace-curtain Irishman.

Wherever there was a point of interest in our travels, Mr. Drew insisted that I see it. He took me to art galleries, Shaker communities, Niagara Falls. He also presented me with Kipling's *Jungle Books* and *Kim*.

Mr. Drew was ever concerned with stimulating my mind and enriching my spirit. I often found it difficult to rest my weary body, since he was utterly indifferent to the cast's accommodations. In every town, large or small, the star's arrival would be heralded with much fanfare, and the leading family or official would offer him a house or royal suite in which to stay.

I remember a small town in upstate New York, where we were informed at the depot that the one hotel did not have a single room available. We were in the midst of a blizzard, and our star was whisked away from the dinky station in a Pierce-Arrow touring car, its isinglass sides buttoned down to protect the gentleman. As he waved *au revoir* to us peasants, we stood fighting over the few taxis, turning blue from the cold, gasping for breath in the face of the raging wind.

Mother and I, along with Jessie Glendening and statuesque Rose Winter, who played the roué's mistress, and Helen Collier, the general understudy who eventually became another roommate back in New York, were forced to hire an open horse-drawn sleigh in which we started our search for shelter.

Show folk were considered undesirables in those days. Actors were one step above lepers unless they were Drews or Bernhardts, so we rode for what seemed like hours, our mufflers wrapped around our frozen faces, being turned away from one rooming house after another. At last, some cautious landlady recommended a tavern, which turned out to be a saloon. That's where we slept—over a saloon, the four of us.

It couldn't have been uglier, but mercurial Brownie couldn't be depressed for long. It was all so dreadful that she found it funny. Anyway, the smell of good draft beer was wafting up to our cell through the cracks in the floor, along with the noises in the bar.

Quite sensibly, she called the bartender. When he arrived, she handed him the out-sized pitcher which was in the room and laughed, "We will have some beer, Innkeeper—as much as this will hold. We have need to lift our spirits."

The other ladies joined us and we happily talked shop and made another theatrical memory, while my three companions drank that immense pitcher empty. It cost ten cents and helped the grown-ups share a child's deep winter sleep.

Mr. Drew took us out for a sleigh ride the next day and never even asked where we were staying. It was clear that one simply made do—and we did. At the theatre, our dressing rooms had no doors. Mr. Drew did order sheets to be hung over the entrances to give the ladies privacy, but there was no running water and we washed in basins filled with melted ice. I remember no bathroom. It was indeed the far reaches of the Empire—the last outpost. But it was theatre.

When the *Prodigal* tour was to end, Mr. Drew closed our show in Washington, D.C., "in order to see you home properly, Childey." And that he did, breaking my heart in the doing. He might just as well have said, "Get thee to a nunnery."

I was back at Sacred Heart after a short stay at Central High School, where I went out with boys for the first time and almost died of stage fright. No one has ever suffered such torture. I had no patter, no small talk—nor big talk for that matter—and absolutely no poise, despite Miss Minnie Hawke's past efforts in Washington. If a boy held my hand, my throat closed up, shutting off all air. The vaguest suggestion of a lad's interest produced shock and guilt in me.

Reality was such a jungle—with no signposts, landmarks, or boundaries.

Not so very long ago, a serious and marvelous young actress, with whom I was playing a scene on Broadway, walked off the stage during a performance. Like all of us, she lives in terror. Like some of us who have not been helped sufficiently, she succumbs to it. The demarcation between mobility and paralysis is a thread.

John Drew was a gigantic ego. His statement was so elaborate that any child not understanding the language could interpret what was going on. This young lady is all shadows and nuance and not one speck of ego. In her honest search for inner meaning, in her tortuous self-examination and her compulsion to work at genius level at all times, she strips herself of all protective covering and she exposes her nerve ends. Frightened out of her wits, she walks on the stage with all guards down, the most vulnerable of creatures.

Actor's fear is an occupational disease, and one learns to live with it. This is the greatest contribution a teacher can make—the strength to control this fear.

I wonder how many people realize the importance of health and energy in the performing arts. My colleague was originally worried about the critics on opening night. When Brooks Atkinson raved about her beautiful work, her next terror was the letdown the audience might feel after what she apparently considered his hyperbole. She trembled through the weeks and when we were to play an Actor's Benefit performance—certainly the most generous of audiences—she went into a complete decline.

I sat backstage with her. This shining talent who had whispered her part all through rehearsals, afraid that the rest of the cast would hear her imagined inadequacies and hold her in contempt, now hoarsely confessed her panic.

"They're going to say, 'Is *this* what she got those notices for?'"

"Nonsense," I scolded. "They'll adore you. If anything, your performance has grown richer since the opening."

"I'll be a mess that night—I know it. I'll be a mess, a mess!"

"Even if you're not in top form, they'll love you. Now stop this."

There are times when we cannot help each other, no matter how much we try. I wasn't being particularly kind to the girl. Simply and selfishly, I wanted her to be good. My work is better when I play with a fine actor in fine form. It suffers in the presence of inexperience or inadequacy. An actor is spurred by talent, stimulated by the excitement of a real challenge.

In my youth, I became very distressed when I had to work with less than good actors. In an effort to compensate, there would be a flood of energy and broadening of gesture that would unbalance the whole work. It was a terrible trait and I had to get rid of it.

When I reached a position that allowed me to make demands, one thing I always insisted on was the perfect actor for the part—the best cast available. Good actors sparking each other make for the wild fire that lights up the theatre. This young woman was such an artist. But her nerve ends are raw—her agony is not occasional, but endless.

My young friend started missing performances here and there, and one night while we were playing a scene I watched her blur and drift off like an FM station. First it was her attention. Her body soon followed.

My heart sank. *Where is she going?* I thought. The audience—innocent of any change in business—sat along with me wondering the same thing.

I improvised. "Come back, Dear—I haven't finished talking to you yet."

She ignored me and just kept going. I was alone on that stage. Disaster seemed certain. I didn't know what to do. If I improvised dialogue or action to explain her behavior her next move might totally invalidate it. I just waited. An eternity seemed to go by. I heard a scuffle in the wings and the young lady was suddenly catapulted onto the stage.

"I went up to see how Stephen was," she answered sweetly.

The play went on, and I hope she does. The theatre needs actresses of her quality. But she is a candle in the wind. She was given no guard to protect her flame. It could have happened to me, but I was lucky. I had Brownie, and I fell under most congenial influences. One might say my stars were in conjunction.

6

I T wasn't until I worked with William Gillette in *Dear Brutus* that I saw for the first time a combination of presence and dimension, substance and shadow. Here was a man who created his truth out of complete technique. His intelligence and control were remarkable, and his instincts never deceived him. I was never again to see such timing as this man had; it was eery.

He knew exactly—to a fraction of a second—how long a pause could be held for the greatest possible effect. His rapport with the audience was extrasensory; his power over the spectator, supreme; the mastery of his natural gifts, astonishing.

There was great simplicity to his style, and style in his simplicity. Never in the least florid, he was always real and seemingly spontaneous. Rex Harrison today has much the same silken quality. It is a felicitous combination of grain and polish. It was all so neat and effortless—to the beholder.

Just being on the same stage with him for one evening was equal to a full dramatic course.

William Gillette was the son of a United States senator, and was once both friend and secretary to Mark Twain. A tall, slender man who was playwright and actor, Mr. Gillette had a keen intelligence. He was tweedy and professorial—the perfect Sherlock Holmes, a part which he had written for himself and played repeatedly and with such astonishing success that it was difficult to disassociate him from the role. Indeed, at rehearsals, with his meerschaum pipe in hand, his blue hawk's eye on every detail, his fine, aquiline nose sniffing for clues, searching for his truth, I half expected him to get out his violin and hypodermic needle.

Early in rehearsal, when the English director Iden Paine complained of my accent and testily announced that he did not understand my speech, I became speechless. I was certain I was going to be fired.

"She simply has a slight southern accent," Mr. Gillette observed, as if it were a Holmesian deduction. He gave me Shakespeare's sonnets to read aloud until that problem was conquered.

Dissatisfied with Mr. Paine's handling of me, Mr. Gillette secretly took things into his own hands. For the whole last week of rehearsal, Mr. Gillette and I had nightly clandestine meetings in Alf Hayman's office atop the Empire Theater. Mr. Hayman was now head of the Frohman Enterprise. In his office Mr. Gillette would undo all the work of the day. Not without some mischief, he told me to follow Mr. Paine's instructions during rehearsals and later ignore him—on opening night I was to play our scenes as *we* were now doing.

It was inevitable that this deception would not only be eventually revealed but take its toll as well. Opening night in Atlantic City was a disaster. I was dashed against the rocks in my attempt to sail through Scylla and Charybdis. It was just awful.

One could hardly blame the director for the endless list of criticisms he handed me when the final curtain came down, but I was plunged into deep depression and, with Mother, fled from the theatre. I walked her feet off as we tramped the boardwalk, and I almost choked on saltwater taffy as I pondered over all my mistakes. All my choices had been wrong. I felt no truth in anything I had done. I didn't believe in my Margaret. How could I have expected anyone else to?

When Mother got me to return to the hotel, afraid I'd catch pneumonia, there in the lobby was the wonderful and patient Mr. Gillette.

"I've been waiting for you, 'Dream Daughter.' I have a message from our producer. Alf Hayman said to tell you that he is prouder than ever of his little leading lady—and by the way, my dear—so am I."

Mr. Hayman would have had to be mad to be proud of me that night, but it didn't matter. Both men seemed to understand the transition I was in, and hope and resolve replaced futility.

Mr. Paine kept his distance the rest of the week. His only suggestions were in staging and, slowly, everything began to fall into place for me.

By the time we opened in Washington, it was going better. Mr. Gillette was wholly confident. Each night he dropped me a note and we visited, never discussing the part but always having such a delightful time that my first buoyant entrance with him was made on a wave of genuine, light-hearted affection.

Our December opening in New York was everything Mr. Gillette promised, and my recognition in the press the finest Christmas present I ever received. Even the acid Dorothy

Parker was kind to an extreme. I was drunk on all the glorious things I was reading about myself and by the time I arrived at the theatre the next evening I knew them all by heart. Then came the jolt. Mr. Gillette called me into his dressing room. He told me never to allow anyone to corrupt my simplicity and made a point of warning me about the newspaper reviews.

"You see, Helen, I never read them and you shouldn't either. They can only be destructive. Anything that *can* be changed to help you will be quickly told you by your director after *he* has read the criticism. Let him make the correction —if you see it in print, it's so hurtful! As for the good things, they only make you self-conscious."

It's true that detailed praise can corrupt, and to this day I don't like to hear compliments about specific moments. I become self-conscious and lose freedom. I once actually ruined an exit in *Clarence* this way.

When I met the critic Ashton Stevens, he was amazed that I had never read his reviews of me, and when I explained why, he laughed and told me the definitive story that proved Mr. Gillette's point.

Ashton Stevens had raved about Ethel Barrymore in some play or other. It seemed that she had read the line, "We are all alone in this empty house!" with such final sibilance that she evoked—according to the critic—such emptiness as he never dreamed possible. He just waxed poetic about that sibilance. The following week, when he returned to the theatre for a second helping, Miss Barrymore was hissing like a cobra.

If I fared well with Mr. Gillette, it was because, with his help, I appeared as ingenuous as I really was.

* * *

There are no star-makers any more on Broadway—men

who can take the long view and gamble on the development of a talent. It was Hollywood that started doing this, after changing economics made it impossible on Broadway. It was the picture studio that found a young actor or actress, put him under long-term contract, and launched a campaign of study and grooming.

Seeds of talent emerged as cinematic giants, actors and actresses of heroic adequacy. With the aid of brilliant technicians, Pygmalion-like cosmeticians, coaches, and directors, bright and lasting stars were created. When a goddess like Greta Garbo had every facet of her genius polished to its finite point, there was no stopping her short of the zenith.

Yes, it was the picture studios and men like Irving Thalberg, at MGM, who became the star-makers. But long before, when I was a girl on Broadway, it was the Charles Frohmans and the George C. Tylers who created long-lasting careers. I guess I was born at the right time. I was helped by all three.

It was my usual luck, after the Gillette show, that the Broadway producer George C. Tyler took an interest in me. After casting me as the touring *Pollyanna,* he watched my work and decided to take me under his wing. I became his protegée and, for the first time, had a professional home and a semblance of security. On plain faith, with no written contract, Mr. Tyler took over my career, buying and even commissioning plays for me.

He had presented Sarah Bernhardt, Eleanora Duse, George Arliss, and Laurette Taylor. Young newcomers included Alfred Lunt, Jeanne Eagels, and Lynn Fontanne. I was certainly in excellent company and good hands, but I also could have been a novitiate in a convent. There was an endless list of do's and don'ts and never any argument.

George C. Tyler was the last of the Victorians. He was ageless, squat, and pink. He could, from the waist up, have been a portrait by Raeburn, but he was bowlegged and he barreled along, making pronouncements that he made certain were heeded. His word was law; his slightest suggestion, an edict. His disfavor was too terrible to contemplate, no less incur. I will be grateful always to this stern guardian. Everything he did was for my good, if not my joy. There were times when I felt we were playing the Father and the Daughter in *The Barretts of Wimpole Street.*

Mr. Tyler spent great sums on productions and certain names, but he could be penurious about small things. One of the smallest, many of his actors believed, was the salaries he paid. It never occurred to me to complain. It occurred to others, but rare was the creature who would stand up to Mr. Tyler. Alfred Lunt was as timid as I about such matters, but Lynn Fontanne—not yet Mrs. Lunt—was not only a rare creature, but outraged for both Alfred and herself.

Though Lynn was hardly the grand duchess she is today, as far back as I can remember she always had authority and a wardrobe. She got herself announced to His Nibs and swept past the secretary, materializing before our producer.

She was framed in the doorway, a figure of tragic dimension, a portrait of a muse. "Mr. Tyler," she declaimed, with her impeccable attention to every syllable.

Mr. Tyler was studying a script and smoking one of his Havana cigars.

"Mr. Tyler!" she now repeated, as she grew taller in stature and heroic impatience.

"Yes, yes!" he bellowed with irritation. "What do you want?"

Mr. Tyler puffed his Havana, and Lynn's hopes went up in smoke. She could have been a petitioner at the court of Ivan the Terrible. She backed out, thanking him for his many kindnesses in employing her, for paying her anything at all, and for allowing her to stay in the country.

I don't know how she even went as far as the door. The valor of the girl! I remained this side of the threshold, the obedient little girl who always did what she was told.

Now he began throwing books at me. Each was like a prescription from the stern family doctor. Dumas *père*, in his entirety, was to prepare me for an appreciation of France. Mr. Tyler loved France. The works of William Allen White, the Emporia, Kansas, editor, were to insure my appreciation of the American scene. I was never encouraged to read anything for the sheer pleasure of it, not even O. Henry. I laughed anyway.

*   *   *

At this time, biography became my great love. Actors' biographies, of course. When I was very young, I half believed one could find within the pages of these memoirs the key to greatness. It's rather like trying to find the soul in the map of the human body. But it is enlightening—and it does solve some of the mysteries.

I began my biographies with J. Forbes-Robertson—that first Hamlet of mine, whom Mother had taken me to see in Washington. Forbes-Robertson's father, I learned, was a London *Times* art critics, and the lad had been encouraged to become a painter. His generation's greatest Hamlet insisted in his book that he did not enjoy acting and felt temperamentally unsuited to the theatre. He remained both unsuited and acclaimed throughout his brilliant acting career.

That was a lesson, I think. Despite all of our protests, most of us end up doing exactly what we really want and probably attracting those catalysts that will bring it about.

Mr. Gillette once told me a story of a small boy who was a mathematical genius—a true prodigy, who awed everyone but his parents. They were petrified of him. His wife was so totally involved with equations that his parents feared monomania. In an effort to help them, Mr. Gillette suggested that they take the child to the theatre in order to divert him and stimulate his imagination. With this end in mind, he presented them with tickets to Maude Adams' *Peter Pan.*

The anxious mother and father now sat in the theatre watching their son with gratitude and relief. He was obviously and utterly engrossed.

When intermission came, they happily asked how he liked the play.

"Do you know?" the boy answered. "There were 71,832 words in that act."

We are what we are, and I suppose we just have to accept ourselves and others.

The theatre is filled with actors who detest acting. But not quite enough to give it up, I have observed. How often I myself have proclaimed my fatigue and the never-diminishing doubts. Acting is such an onerous chore and I certainly don't have to prove myself any longer. Why do I keep subjecting myself to all the pressure and the indignities?

I dream of fleeing to my house in Cuernavaca where there are no headlines, no deadlines. Why don't I do it? I can afford it. Why don't I just quit? Why, indeed? Because true actors are incurable seekers.

I'm inquisitive. I was born inquisitive and I'll die inquisitive. I'm even inquisitive now about death. There's still so much I don't know—so much that could be judiciously employed in my life's work once I learned it.

❃ ❃ ❃

Of the many biographies I read in my youth—and I read them avidly—one of the most impressive was that of Lisa Felix, the astonishing French actress known throughout the world simply as Rachel.

Born in terrible poverty, an urchin who sang in the streets

of Paris with her sister for the small coins thrown at her feet, it is not surprising that she became the cold and grasping woman her biography describes. In her short life, her many relationships were utterly reprehensible—not for their passionate involvement but for lack of it. She was as shallow as she was greedy.

Over the bed in her damasked lair, her current and wealthy lover—when his attention was allowed to wander—came face to face with the very guitar she used to play when, as a gamin, she sang *La Marseillaise* in the gutters of Chaillot. She sang it so stirringly that she was lifted out of obscurity by Charon, the famous teacher, and placed in the *Conservatoire* from which she graduated to the *Gymnase* and then to *La Comédie Française,* where she reigned supreme. And it all started with that guitar.

Rachel was already a legend in her lifetime and when she was through with a romance, the lover always wanted the guitar both as a souvenir and proof of their intimacy. Rachel's upraised palms spoke eloquently of her reluctance to part with such a keepsake. After using every other means of persuasion, the man would then offer to buy it. But *la petite guitare* was priceless—without the price—she would insist. Monsieur le prince or comte or baron would then say with Gaelic logic that *le rien* is without the price and Rachel —ever the realist—would be forced to agree. This woman had all the ethics of a boa constrictor and all the guitars her walnut *armoires* could hold, every single one of them the very same with which she had accompanied herself on that historic day she had first been discovered. This artiste was in the guitar business on the side.

The incomparable *Phaedra,* Rachel was, by consensus, the greatest tragedienne of her age. I was fascinated that this vulgar, superficial creature could, from all the written evidence, plumb the depths of emotion and sing so profoundly and beautifully Racine's fine words.

Rachel, though fancy-free, to be sure, evidently was still subject to the ties of blood. When her adored sister died, friends came to her house to inform her of the tragedy. On hearing the terrible news, she fell in a dead faint and could not be revived for quite some minutes. When she regained consciousness and found herself lying on a chaise, she realized what had transpired and became extremely agitated. Her genuine grief was replaced by her professional need to examine it. Her companions began to console her but she sat up and shouted, "What did I do? How did I fall? Did I distort my face in any way? Tell me!"

She had truly loved her sister and she had truly fainted, but she was an actress. That special eye. That insatiable curiosity. It is both terrible and marvelous.

❊ ❊ ❊

The old-fashioned idea that the simple piling up of experiences, one on top of another, can make you an artist, is, of course, so much rubbish. If acting were just a matter of experience, then any busy harlot could make Garbo's *Camille* pale.

Kay Laurell—a tigress of a woman who had appeared with me in a play—was, in life, one of the great *femmes fatales*. It did nothing for her acting. Actually, Kay was famous for posing in the Ben Ali Haggin tableaux naked to the waist.

If young ladies did not move on stage, they could be naked quite legally. Discovering this loophole, Broadway was suddenly filled with living pictures—those rococo, neo-Oriental tableaux.

There on stage at the *Follies* were Ziegfeld's most divine

beauties, powdered and rouged from head to toe, and in all their glory. Since Kay had more glory than anyone else, she was usually dead center, the figurehead on the Ship of Beauty or Pure Delight. Whatever it was, she always proved an eye-filling spectacle.

Kay was a statuesque girl of considerable beauty. Her protector at the time was Reginald Vanderbilt, and they made quite a glamorous couple about town until, in a startling substitution, Vanderbilt was replaced by Clarence Darrow. Already generously endowed, Kay was given even greater substance by her association with the great lawyer. When she was in her late and fulsome thirties, she became a legitimate actress.

One day around Christmas time, Mother and I went to her apartment for eggnog, and I was astonished. The whole flat was out of a Nita Naldi film; there was actually a large ermine throw on her busy bed. For a change of pace, there on the grand piano was a bust of Mr. Darrow.

Kay was in a rage when we arrived and had, that Yuletide afternoon, little or no goodwill toward men. She was screaming and throwing things across the room as quickly as her French maid could retrieve them. They were gifts, it seems, from an unofficial admirer. Silk scarves, beaded bags, and lace handkerchiefs—all of them exquisite—were flung in every direction. She was not a warm-hearted woman. They were gifts all right. Gifts that she didn't believe fit her station. The most expensive were in "the low hundreds." They were not what this glittery-eyed houri was accustomed to.

"That goes back where it came from," she was shouting. "And that! What the hell is he trying to be—*charming?* With all these *cute* things! He knows I wouldn't accept such bagatelle! Out! Back it goes. It is an insult!"

We watched her fill the room with Christmas cheer until

she was hoarse. She wasn't very sentimental, but I thought her marvelous. She was authentic. The skull and crossbones were right out there on the label for all to see. She was rather like Cleopatra to me, and higher judges than I showed mercy on her.

Kay settled down eventually when she married a rich South American and moved to Brazil. She became a Catholic convert, and a devout one.

Though she had one of the most luxuriant accouchements on record, she nevertheless died in childbirth. Her faith thus assured her a place in Paradise. Kay never became a star but she landed in Heaven anyway. I will never forget her. She was very swell, was Kay Laurell. And she called Detroit *"De Trois."*

It is not the facts of life alone that give you understanding, but your deep responses to them. There is a special eye that an artist must have. Rachel had it. Kay, with all her experience, did not.

*   *   *

I joined the APA-Phoenix to work for the first time in repertory. I've reached the stage where I love to play small character roles that can illuminate the corners of a playwright's world. Cameos, gems that beg for experience but do not demand the responsibilities of stardom.

The flattering, if arbitrary, label, First Lady of the Theatre, takes its toll. The demands are great, not only in energy but eventually in dramatic focus. It is difficult, if not impossible, for a star to occupy an inch of space without bursting seams, cramping everyone else's style and unbalancing a play. No matter how self-effacing a famous player may be, he makes an entrance as a casual neighbor and the audience interest shifts to the house next door.

After several roles with the APA, the company decided to

revive George Kelly's 1925 play, *The Show Off*, with me as the mother. It was certainly the right part at the right time, a miracle of dovetailing. What a glorious bonus this successful revival has been for me.

Anyway, the Lunts recently came back one night after a performance and Lynn pointed her finger at me accusingly as she entered the dressing room.

"That isn't acting, Helen—that's *memory*. Memory!"

"You're darn tootin'!" I answered.

And she was right. As I had studied my role of Mrs. Fisher in *The Show Off*, I had used Aunt Mamie mercilessly. I could hear the Hayes sisters, Mamie and Essie, sitting around the table at home in Washington as they reported their encounters with hapless friends.

These victims were always portrayed as fools or fishwives. My dear Aunt Mamie always came off as a figure of great dignity and compassion. All I had to do was let Aunt Mamie move in. But so completely did she take over that at rehearsals, alarmingly near our opening, I was still expressing myself in her words instead of the author's. When I was supposed to prophesy tartly of my spoiled and demanding daughter that she would be "sadly left," instead, out popped Aunt Mamie again, with, "She'll have another think coming." She had become my Irish dybbuk.

I was married for over 30 years to a playwright, and an author's words mean a great deal to me. And so, in exasperation, I called up to the peanut gallery which is the nearest in theatre to Heaven, "O.K., Aunt Mamie. Thanks for all your help, but will you please get off the stage so I can get on with it?"

My director, Stephen Porter, and the rest of the cast looked out at the empty theatre and thought I'd gone mad. But that was my release from the madness.

I wish I could muster the courage to pass on some of the things I've learned. Time was when older actors felt free to speak up and spread their experience around like plant food for the seedling. Until I studied with Frances Robinson Duff, my only school was backstage, my only teachers experienced performers. But these days we feel odd about speaking. Often, at rehearsal I am tempted to make a suggestion, but I resist it. In my day, bless them, one's elders never shut up. If you are made receptive to advice and help and example early in life, you remain open and responsive for the rest of it.

One of the rare times I felt unqualified satisfaction with myself was on the set of *White Sister* with Clark Gable. We were having a performance problem and were in such a muddle that our director, Victor Fleming, said, "Let's break and clear our heads."

We scattered, each of us trying to recharge, to gather our wits. I had just flopped into my chair when one of the lighting men climbed down from his parapet and approached me. His bird's-eye view had given him a perspective lost to those of us milling around in the arena.

"Miss Hayes, you and Mr. Gable are not doing that scene right." He then proceeded to tell me why. I was impressed with his opinion but much more impressed that he had come to me. He knew instinctively that I would listen. I had been listening greedily since I was five years old.

When I auditioned for the western road company of *Pollyanna*, Patricia Collinge, who had played it on Broadway and was going to take the play through New England, said to me: "That's lovely, my dear. Only you must learn to play the part without crying." I had still to learn what Fanny Brice told me years later. "If *you* cry, honey, they don't!"

And it was a character woman in *Pollyanna* who saw how

rigid my body became when I felt insecure on stage. I can't remember her name, but never forgot her advice.

"When you feel nervous and want to tense something, curl your toes, Dearie. They're inside your shoes and nobody will see what you're doing."

I spent years curling my toes and was forever grateful, though it did cramp my insteps occasionally. When I remembered to curl my toes, I stopped hunching my shoulders.

I treasure the second-hand dramatic course from Sarah Bernhardt that supplemented my studies with Frances Robinson Duff. In the years during which Jean Dixon lived with us, sharing my room as a sister, she led me through Rostand's *L'Aiglon* in French. Jean had studied with Madame in Paris, and this had been one of their exercises.

The speeches, as in all French classical drama, were inordinately long, and I was having trouble. Then Jean told me that the Divine Sarah had a divine device. When studying a role, she always underscored the key words of a sentence or the key phrases of a long declamation. She told her students, "All you have to do is say these very important words clearly; then you must *race* through the rest to avoid being heavy and boring. One must *never* be boring! The audience will not lose any of the meaning and will understand the whole speech. Of course, they really won't," she now added, "but they will *think* they do, and that is the whole illusion."

How often I've cringed at rehearsal when I've heard a young actor boom, "*Oh how I wish . . .*" and then dribble off into a mumble, leaving us forever ignorant of what he was so ardently wishing for. This is one of the common failings of young actors.

Complaints about inaudibility have become chronic, but inaudibility is only the symptom. The real trouble is an untrained ear, untrained to hear the melody of speech.

Sometimes on stage, my mind fairly shrieks, "For God's sake, get the tune right."

My acting lessons have run the gamut from Sarah Bernhardt to my poodle dog.

7

In 1920, Mr. Tyler commissioned an adaptation of Mary Roberts Rinehart's Bab diaries to be written for me, removing me from the happy cast of *Clarence*. I was torn from Alfred Lunt, who had replaced Vernon Castle as my idol. I had such a crush on him—but that was epidemic. I think the company got on so well because all hostility was reserved for the beauteous Miss Fontanne, who visited him nightly.

I was extremely happy playing Cora, the flapper, and it seemed cruel to snatch me from the bosom of this new family. The company was furious with Mr. Tyler, which was exactly like shaking a fist at the heavens. Though he was only 45, I believed Mr. Tyler was older than God; he believed himself to be as omniscient. He "gave-eth" and he "took-eth" away.

My last performance was heartbreaking. A snowstorm was

raging but hadn't discouraged the enthusiastic crowds that jammed the Hudson nightly. It was the last time that I would play that brilliant comedy with that congenial cast. The last time I would hear that glorious laughter flood the theatre. The last time I would hear Alfred play the saxophone so terribly.

Bab made a charming vehicle for me, and our successful opening in Taunton, Massachusetts, only vaguely suggested the personal triumph I was to have in Boston. That Hollis Street Theatre opening, the brilliant critical reception, and the months that followed were unforgettable.

As Bab, I upset the entire student body at Harvard, to Mother's surprise as well as my own. I could have been Beerbohm's Zuleika Dobson for the fuss I caused. The stage door was always crowded—if not with Billy Coupier's white-tied pillars of society, certainly with their lettered, sweatered sons. A steady stream of candy, flowers, and golden hearts flooded the theatre. After the first senior dance at the Copley Plaza, notes were forever being pushed under our hotel door —invitations to tea dansants and after-theatre suppers. With my new white chiffon dress, my cream-colored velvet cape and feather fan, I was prepared to accept each and every one.

I was in seventh heaven. As Bab, I was having my first burst of personal popularity, and I impatiently awaited the confidence that should have gone along with it. For the first time, boys were competing for my attention. The literature majors were writing sonnets to Bab. The art minors were painting and sculpting her portrait. Biology students were dreaming of Bab.

Babism had taken over Harvard. In every subject, the boys were cutting classes in order to attend repeated matinees. They were failing test after test in order to see her. It was divine.

Naturally, I was diverted by all this campus activity. Mother noticed the new shine in my eyes, the flush in my cheek, and realized that my rapid climb to the heights of the theatre could—without her—be diverted into the popular turkey trot which was just Bab's speed. I felt like a sub-deb and simply relished the life that had opened up to me. There were even a couple of boys who liked me—one in particular who presented a problem.

I was always easily swayed by fun and now, with all this flattery, I was fairly floating. But Brownie didn't believe in floating. Floating meant passivity. Mother knew the shortest distance between two points and she never, for a single moment, forgot exactly where we were going. Though I did. As captain, she pulled rank often. At this point in my life, especially, she allowed no weaving, no cruising. She kept me smack on course.

I'm afraid I resented her interference and her power. I was not without the same rebellious spirit that had driven her from Grandfather Hayes's domination; but unlike her, I never revolted. Evidently, I didn't really want to. Brownie had all the singleness of purpose, all the fierce will, that I lacked, and she was utterly committed and dedicated to my future. Without her, I might have laughed, tossed my head, and danced my way right off the stage.

And so Mother sorted out all the invitations in Boston, taking charge as she did in everything. She reminded me that I was a working actress who wasn't used to this kind of social life and that my work would suffer if I—as she put it —"plunged into a whirl of gaiety."

She accepted only those invitations she felt valuable or innocuous. In any event, she always came along, keeping her eagle eye open, and contributing the fun and easy companionship that Bab promised but found so difficult to deliver. Escorts always adored her; and Mother, once she was sure that she had everything under control, enjoyed herself thoroughly. There were so many different boys around that she felt that there was safety in numbers. She kept saying that anyway.

It was somehow poetic justice that Mary Roberts Rinehart's son, Alan, was one of the Crimson students affected by the Bab fever. Alan was as bewildered by his youth as I was by mine. After seeing me in the play 25 times, he asked me to run off to South America with him. This didn't seem sufficient reason to leave the country, and on further musing it occurred to me that with his filial connection he must have been attending the Hollis Theatre on passes, a conjecture that somehow diminished his passion if not his endurance. Dear Alan. He was such a puppy and so in love with love. He wanted to be an author and started rewriting life very early.

Young Rinehart was tall and skinny, a long drink of water spiked with a drop from a chum's flask. When we danced together, we did not resemble the Castles. We could more easily have suggested the future Hartmanns, only *we* didn't mean to be funny. I came up to the first onyx stud on his moiré evening vest; and on a fairly populated floor, Alan looked as if he were dancing alone. When the other couples cleared away, there we were, the long and short of it. Nonetheless, he was one of our frequent escorts to those teas, dances, and senior club Saturday evenings at the Copley Plaza that Mother accepted. She was always my companion. We could have been a young lady of Spain and her duenna.

One night, Alan, after a single small glass of homemade port, decided to transform our foxtrot into what turned into a kind of apache dance. I was swung around the room, my new red satin slippers never touching the floor. My skinny, dramatic partner was making a scene that he could later enjoy regretting.

I was rescued by one of the other lads, and the long-suffering Alan was now able to write me a note the next day that began, "Dear Helen: Last night I was drunk at the ball. I cannot bear to see you in the arms of another man."

He was truly authored by his mother. He apologized to Brownie and with her amused sanction I agreed to take a "stroll in the Common" with him. It was a warm day and I was parched with thirst. As I affectionately remember it, we strolled in what I am sure Alan later described as a pregnant silence.

"Helen!" he suddenly blurted out.

"Yes, Alan."

"Come to Peru with me."

"Peru? Did you say Peru?"

"Yes, Peru!"

"But I thought you came from Sewickley, Pennsylvania."

"I do. But Mother's there. Peru's the place."

"The place for what?"

"For llamas and Inca ruins and Lake Titicaca. You've got to come to Peru, Helen."

"I'm dying of thirst, Alan. May I have some Moxie?"

"Gee whizz, Helen," he said, turning his pockets inside out. "I've only got 15¢ and—well, I've gotta get back to Cambridge."

* * *

Mother liked Alan and was charmed by his gangling intensity. She also knew that, though I was fond of him, he wasn't a threat. She was not so certain of another swain. This young man stood tall among the others. Not given to extravagance of expression, his declarations of love were as conservative as his name. He made it apparent, however, that he was serious. He was interested in marriage.

Brownie was put to a double test when the boy's aunt sent us a very formal invitation to tea. A Marquand dowager, the lady was a most prominent Bostonian. Though Mother was awed, she knew immediately why we were being summoned. It had never occurred to me.

Evidently, my young suitor had told his family about me and his frightened mother, far from Boston, had asked her sister to investigate this "little actress" and her ambitious mother. It was to be the classic scene in which the lady would ever so subtly pave the little chippie's way out of the young aristocrat's life. English kings and Brahmin princes might cavort with actresses *but* they didn't marry them. Mother was convinced this could be the only reason why the society leader asked us—since her nephew was not invited to join us.

I was amazed. In the first place, there was no serious consideration of his proposal, though that *is* one question a girl could ponder indefinitely. When Mother got through writing her true romance, I was livid. But Brownie insisted on accepting what she felt to be a challenge. She was ready for a contest. I was going to be the tennis ball at a Wimbledon match.

After Mother carefully chose our costumes for the occasion, we climbed Beacon Hill that afternoon and arrived at the magnificent house. The dimensions of the marble hall were meant to intimidate, and this was simply the prologue. The butler ushered us into the spacious drawing room where Her Highness sat, multi-reflected in the sterling tea service.

White-haired, a string of enormous pearls glowing on her blue silk dress, the lady was all frosty graciousness. Her hands waved us to petit point chairs and then busied themselves arranging and rearranging the Meissen china, her keen eyes all the while searching for hints of our true character.

She made a ballet of tea and small talk, all arabesques and balances as she flitted from one precious point to another. She was wonderful to study. A sprinkle of remote names and places was a delicate reminder of our two different worlds and the apparent superiority of hers. So far she had really said nothing and I decided that Brownie was wrong. I was coveting a pink petit four and planning to spear it with my fork if I were not offered another helping quickly.

The lady, to my chagrin, replaced her cup and saucer on the table, spelling *fini* to our repast. She touched her unrouged lips with the tiny, embroidered napkin, tilted her head, and barely perceptibly raised her eyebrows. She had the timing of a real pro.

"Mrs. Brown. Let us come to the reason for this meeting. What do you think of this romance between my nephew and your daughter?"

Her polite tone didn't fool Brownie. Brownie, I now knew, couldn't be fooled. Evidently, this was the gambit in a planned game of chess. Mother was supposed to smile and advance her pawn. Eventually, after much delicate war making, castles would tumble and somebody's heart would be broken. Mother was not a chess player, so she knew none of the rules of the game. Her Irish was up and her patience was gone. Brownie's pride equalled any Brahmin's. She might just as well have shattered all the Meissen when she said, "My dear Madam, the sooner my daughter forgets about your nephew and the sooner we can leave Boston, the better."

Our hostess leaned forward in shock and Mother continued, "Helen is an artist. She has a future in the theatre. I *cannot* have it threatened by a meaningless little romance.

And now, I am afraid we must thank you and leave. Helen needs her rest before a performance. . . ."

I was eventually cast on stage as one queen after another. I learned from my mother that day how to play one convincingly.

*   *   *

In Anouilh's *Tiger at the Gates*, there is a beautiful scene, a kind of summit meeting, between the Greek and Trojan generals. Although the shallow Helen of Troy will eventually corrupt the moment, bringing destruction to so many, the cynical dialogue between these men ends in a genuine promise of peace. And all because—as Ulysses readily admits— he has noticed that the lashes on Hector's wife, Andromache, dance upon her cheek in the same enchanting fashion as those on his waiting Penelope. The sudden empathy puts the tawdry political facts in true perspective, dwarfing the reasons for the impending war.

Wise men, star-gazers, and military strategists are helpless in the face of such intangibles. A flick of an eyelash, and war or peace is made.

In Vaughn Williams's —*And So Victoria,* a novel that chronicled those incidents that led to the unlikely ascension of the English monarch, the author postulated that if some minor character, in an out-of-the-way tavern, had not picked his nose, thereby setting off a sequence of events, Victoria would not have become Queen of England. I could not help but further observe that I would not—without his happy gaucherie—have played her and had my greatest theatrical triumph.

So much for reasons. If I had to depend upon the logic of things alone, I should go quite mad.

With none of the historical importance but all of the non

sequitur, Mr. Tyler made me a star when we left Boston to open in New York—and only because a three-named playwright adapted the work of a three-named author and, contractually, the producer could not use one name on the marquee without the other.

EDWARD CHILDS CARPENTER'S
ADAPTATION
OF
MARY ROBERTS RINEHART'S
BAB

was obviously out of the question. And so he planned to put my name up in lights instead of the playwright's.

It was simply a matter of aesthetics. Mother felt so strongly that I was not ready for stardom that she dared, this time, to incur Mr. Tyler's wrath. This was her sole battle with him, and she got out all the ammunition, but she was powerless against his strength. She could not prevail and she was undone by it.

Here was a mother fighting to keep her daughter's name *off* a marquee! Brownie was an original! She wasn't fooled by my Boston Tea Party even if I was. She fought to the very last week but Mr. Tyler never lost a battle. Mother swore that, if my name went up in lights, the star would not be there opening night. When we arrived at the Park Theater in Columbus Circle, there it was on that narrow five-story-high sign:

HELEN
HAYES
IN
BAB

We stood on the island in the middle of the circle, just below the monument, surrounded by the whirling double-decker buses and Checker cabs. I looked over at Mother to see if she was going to carry out her threat, but she was crying. We both just stood there gaping. It is a wonder that the pigeons didn't believe us to be two more statues and light upon our heads.

Yes. The sign was a feast for the eyes and I'd be lying if I didn't admit it. But there were other signs on Broadway that proved Mother right. For one, John Barrymore in *Richard III;* for another, Maxine Elliot in *Trimmed in Scarlet.* There were more: Ruth Chatterton in *Mary Rose,* Pauline Lord in *Samson and Delilah,* George Arliss in *Poldekin,* and my John Drew in *Catbird.* The company I was keeping was sublime. My being one of them was ridiculous.

Mother was right. On opening night, in a desperate effort to live up to that sign out front, I gave one of those shrill, tense performances that became a hazard in my career whenever I was not in top form. I made a botch of the whole business. I couldn't keep it a secret. It was all over the papers the next day.

Heywood Broun, who not so long before had placed me atop a Christmas tree—in a sense making me a star after *Clarence*—now tore me apart. Among other epithets, he called me "cute," which was the unkindest cut of all.

That was the critics' favorite word for me for years, and when they couldn't call me cute any longer without being sued, they changed it to "sweet."

Although not all the newspapers were unkind, I was shattered by Heywood Broun's evaluation of my performance. Shattered because I felt he was right, furious because he *was* right. Mother's silence was eloquent corroboration.

My second-night performance, in reaction, was so understated that the audience thought me in a trance. They were right—I had been living in Never-Never Land. Lew Fields, John Drew, and William Gillette had all warned me never to allow anyone to toy with my gift, never to corrupt my natural style. I was to remain what they all thought was a happy little sunbeam, bouncing about. One would have thought me Tinkerbell, it was all so precious.

They were three wonderful, romantic gentlemen of the old school and I am eternally grateful to them for their priceless training. But they were too kind.

Trading on youth, a sense of fun, and a natural gift, I only started to grow up when the truth sank in—that there are no gifts, that there is a price for everything, and you've got to be willing to pay it.

At 20, I was a veteran actress and—to my mind, at any rate—far from a professional.

8

I SOMETIMES think that if our world ever goes up in smoke, it will not be because of man's Machiavellian evil, but rather his affable incompetence. Inefficiency seems to be running rampant in our world, and our only hope lies in the fact that the wicked so often share this lack of dedication to a job well done. Nature does have its way of compensating.

In all the professions there is a lamentable lack of professionalism. The mere *scanning* of your badly proofread newspaper brings to your attention architects who have forgotten to build staircases to now-inaccessible rooms, surgeons who have either removed the wrong thing, or left hygienic mementoes of their visit, international spies who announce their arrival, and jolly toymakers who break your grandchild's heart on Christmas morn by neglecting to include in the crate the one small part without which the gift cannot be properly assembled.

Pride in workmanship is a sentimental memory, a residue of Victorianism that, along with self-reliance, perseverance, and honesty, form what is now considered the very squarest of life's foundations. All of these qualities are looked down on today with utter contempt unless, of course, one has himself been victimized—the dentist having pulled the wrong tooth.

The reaching out for excellence, the need to be best at what I was doing, I learned from both my mother and my father. Father might have been satisfied with little, but once he had settled for his small place in the world and decided what he was best suited for, he patiently and steadfastly pursued his course. He did his small job well, and with humility, which taught me how to survive success. His middle-class virtues—so cavalierly dismissed today—have been my staff and my strength.

I respect the professional! If he does his job with excellence under trying conditions, one can safely assume that, in life as well, he will behave with fortitude and grace under pressure.

But this is the day of instant genius. Everybody starts at the top, and then has the problem of staying there. Lasting accomplishment, however, is still achieved through a long, slow climb and self-discipline.

I have been harsh with myself and sometimes impatient with others, when we didn't pass muster. Jamie as a small boy had a governess named Miss Fleming, who, blessedly, is still with me—with, alas, only two small poodles as her charges. I recall how she took me to task one day when she found me too stern in my chastisement of my son for some infraction of discipline. He had fallen short of my expectations. Her voice still rings in my ears.

"But, Mrs. MacArthur—he's only a little boy!"

I was taken aback. My eloquent and angry speech was appropriate for a peer. She was right, of course! But Jim grew straight and manly. I cling stubbornly to the notion that I was not wrong in expecting so much of him.

Success had come too easily in my youth. I know too well the dangers of coasting. Success came too early, and too quickly. Instead of carrying me aloft, it was proving to be ballast. I was not only earthbound but, like Carroll's Red Queen, I was moving awfully fast just staying in the same place.

I had never yearned to be an actress—because I always was one. I never dreamed of a career—because I always had one. For 60 years I've heard, "Two minutes, Miss Hayes," and I've sprinted onto the stage. It's become a reflex. Pavlov's actress, that's me.

*   *   *

Once established on Broadway, I started to consolidate a position that most of my peers took years to achieve. Ever so slowly, I approached a more serious view of my life's work.

For quite a while, I had heard and ignored the shrillness of my voice. I also spoke too slowly sometimes. I could hear my voice dragging, almost grinding to a halt. Part of this was a regional drawl I had not completely lost, part of it incorrect breathing, and much of it lack of training. I had not developed control of the tuning device an actor must have inside him.

Slow as my drawling speech could be, I was, in contrast, swift and light of foot. I moved so swiftly I barely touched the ground, and, when I did, I always seemed to be falling down on stage. I fell so often that I actually made up a line to cover the mishap. "Well, I won't get married *this* year," I would say, gaily. Several times this presence of mind earned me applause, faker that I was.

It is remarkable that it took me so long to protect myself. Even when an opening night went well, and the critics were kind enough to call my performance charming, the quality of my playing would decline during the run of a play. I was good one night, less than good the next. There were nights, so Brownie told me, when I wasn't good at all. It never occurred to me that I was not in control of myself, not master of my instrument; but I was unable to replay a melody once caught. My effective performances were luck, catch-as-catch-can.

On tour in *Pollyanna* I started off like a house afire. Across the country my reviews became less and less enthusiastic. I simply could not repeat a good performance at will.

In *Clarence,* there had been an exit that Heywood Broun had generously called one of the three great moments he had experienced in the theatre.

As Cora, the flapper, I was caught up in a pubescent crisis. The archetypical teen-ager, I had blown up a situation to breast-beating tragedy. There I was, carrying on, when my stage father—utterly deflating me—sent me upstairs to wash my face. It was as if Electra, in the midst of her feverish machinations, was told by Aegisthus to go clean her fingernails or shampoo her hair. It was humiliating. Since the teenager's greatest tragedy is the comedy she evokes, Cora's walking papers sent her off the stage in complete shock. As I made my ignominious exit, I kept repeating, "Wash my face, wash my face," in stunned disbelief. It became a dirge for all misunderstood flappers.

First the laughter, and then the applause, lasted so long that I was madly tempted to come back for an encore. This exit actually stopped the show on opening night. Evidently, a whole generation of girls walked up those stairs with me. In a few weeks the gratifying ovation had died down to a smattering of applause and a solitary giggle, and then, to my horror, to absolute silence—absolute and degrading silence. What I had done on opening night was true and instinctive. The audience, recognizing this, repaid me with its pleasure. Now I was trying to recapture that truth, and didn't know how. The attempts became progressively clumsier with increasing desperation.

The whole cast was embarrassed for me, and Mary Boland took me aside one night. She had been one of Mr. Drew's favorite leading women, and she now recalled that she had once found herself in a similar situation.

"I was once made very conscious, dear, of just how funny a certain reading of mine was," she told me. "That, dear, is sheer death. Helen, I beg you, forget how the audience laughed before. Forget how funny it all is. Play it as seriously as you and Cora feel, and the laugh will come back, I promise you—because you'll be spontaneous again. Just stop trying to be funny, dear. It worked for me!"

It was easier said than done. It occurred to me that I might need some real instruction—to go to some kind of school. But all my mentors had warned me against this, and Mother was certain that I would emerge from any class a different girl—artificial and actress-ish.

With Miss Boland's advice, and Brownie's brutally frank dispatch, from her place in the wings, that I was pounding my lines and overplaying those moments I'd been told were particularly funny, I eventually—in an attempt to oil the machinery—forgot about being funny. When I stopped, I found the laughter returned. I thanked Miss Boland and breathed a sigh of relief. I shouldn't have!

It still didn't penetrate that I was powerless to articulate

what I felt, that I was drifting, and that I was just luckily
hitting upon felicitous moments. It didn't penetrate until the
opening night of *Bab*.

Shortly after, Mother and I were asked by Ruth Chatterton to an after-theatre party at Henry Miller's apartment. I
needed cheering up. But it was obvious the moment I came
in that Mr. Broun was not alone in his opinion of my work
in the play. Nobody threw old fruit at me, but actors have
shimmering antennae and I felt the negative vibrations.
Since I respected Ruth Chatterton as an actress as well as a
friend, I asked her what was wrong with my performance.

Ruth was a bluff and a candid woman. She rarely minced
words.

"O.K., Helen. I've always thought you had talent. That's
obvious, and absolutely no credit to you. It's something else."

She now measured a tiny space in the air with her thumb
and forefinger. "You don't have *that* much technique," she
said.

She turned to the soignée Ina Claire, who was listening in
apparent agreement. "How about Frances, Ina? I think she's
just what this youngster needs."

"She's done wonders for me, my dear," Ina confessed.
"She's a marvel! I'll call her *right now. But right this
moment.*"

Ina never stopped her sales talk until she got her party
on the phone. I sat like a frozen robin while these two
women took charge of my life.

It is simply astonishing how, from the very beginning,
people cared and felt that I was worth their trouble. Because
of Ruth's candor and interest, and Ina's kindness and passion
for acting teachers and schools, an appointment was made
immediately. Evidently, there wasn't a moment to be wasted.
The very next afternoon, I was introduced to Frances Robinson Duff and her mother, Madame Duff, who concentrated

on voice projection. They coached Mary Garden and they now became indispensable to me.

* * *

Frances used the Delsart Chart, which was named for a famous French elocutionist. It was based on the proper use of the diaphragm and it enhanced voice production. I learned that only small children know how to breathe correctly. As we grow up and learn less important things at the feet of intellectual masters, we lose this prime talent.

Although the chart was rather precious and some of the diaphragm manipulations, when related to love and hate, struck my funny bone, the greater truth was that I improved immediately. I placed my voice with greater ease, controlled my breathing to such benefit that there was no longer my much-criticized straining and laboring. Vocally, I was released and, for the first time in my theatrical life, I found my voice doing exactly what I wanted with a minimum of argument. We had not always worked that agreeably.

Even more important than this sudden discipline of voice projection was the knowledge that I could really take myself in hand and master all my faculties. In a sense, I started collecting myself.

I blush at the thought of how cute I was all those early years—jumping about and being so fey, sitting on tables instead of chairs, constantly flitting. The charming little girl with the natural sense of make-believe had lost her freshness. She was repeating herself with continuing and corrupting success, until she was 21 and terrible. That's the way it can happen. The Misses Chatterton and Claire saved my professional life with their happy recommendation. Miss Duff became my shadow. For many years, and to the annoyance of many of my directors, she was always at my side on those first rehearsal days of a new play.

There was certainly respectable precedence for this. Bernhardt, Duse, and our shrewd friend Rachel—all the fine European actresses—had coaches who guided them through their great years. When Frances died, I, along with Katharine Hepburn and many others, moved on to Constance Collier, especially when we tackled Shakespeare.

When I once told Miss Collier, who had played in *Peter Ibbetson* with John Barrymore, how successful my early performances had been with John Drew and William Gillette, she smiled.

"My dear, my finest Lady Macbeth was my first—when I was only 19. You see, no one had told me how difficult it was."

I now knew.

It is said that acting cannot be taught—merely learned. And this is true. What can be taught, however, is how to free your channels of expression. It is what Miss Duff promised to do, and did.

Though technique cannot give you the transference to a character, it does not hinder it. There is probably no more spectacular inner experience, midst all the chaos of rehearsals, than that moment of truth when you first became the part and lose yourself in it. The character is infused with a life of its own and the mystery humbles one.

You can be taught by the right teacher to open yourself to this experience. You can be taught by the right teacher to use best what you already have at your command. How to use your voice more effortlessly, your arms more gracefully, your body more meaningfully. You can be taught to conserve your breath and ration your energy. Talent may not be for sale, but the best way to package and display your gift is.

Other things that cannot be given you, I believe, are your choices, that is, exactly the way you are going to convey or express what the author means to say. In other words, when you are all at sea, the school can give you the craft that keeps you afloat. Once you choose your course, the craft then cuts through the waves, prepared to follow it.

*   *   *

Lillian Gish once said that fine acting is made up of three things: talent, taste, and temperament. I suppose one can replace these words with intuition, choices, excitement. How does an actor say what he wants to say in the best possible manner? There are countless ways to convey irritation or delight, grief or joy. First, one must do it as the character and then in the most pithy and attractive manner. Even unattractive qualities must be—in an odd way—made attractive. For instance, playing a dullard, the actor must bore other characters in the cast, but never the audience.

Now it stands to reason that, the larger the artist's emotional investment, the more impressive his wealth of understanding, the more varied will be those choices. Still, once that choice is made—and this belongs solely in the province of the artist—he must still have been trained sufficiently to articulate it. Craft and navigator!

Once I exposed myself to study, my need for training led me to the most diverse tutors. One of Charlie's good friends was the socialite polo player Tommy Hitchcock. I studied boxing with his trainer, Joe Fitton, for two years, until I could move like featherweight Benny Leonard. I then went on to fencing, with a French master; and to interpretive dancing with Florence Fleming Noyes.

Miss Noyes was influenced by Isadora Duncan, and we pupils were taught to dance barefooted and in little chiffon shifts. We were very pure and looked like fugitives from a Grecian urn. Sometimes we were vagabond autumn leaves, adrift and at the mercy of the four winds. And sometimes we were wavelets, lapping at the shore—and sometimes even the shore, appalled by the impertinence of the lapping wavelets.

As most religions share like tenets, so do dramatic schools have a certain catholicity. I have seen such ritual in Strasberg's methodism. Was it all St. Stanislavski? If you are an inquisitive actor, and not just a paid-up member of Equity, you investigate all the schools. I've not missed any.

Certainly, anything that stretches the imagination is desirable, but one can be diverted from serious progress. At Miss Noyes's, one day, we were supposed to be seals sunning ourselves on an ice floe. This was all very well, but a zealous and obese classmate became so carried away with the conceit that she rolled right on top of me. I fear that I did not at all feel like clapping my flippers with camaradie. I didn't feel in the least like another seal being chummy. I felt like me being crushed by a fat lady and I disengaged myself as quickly as I could.

This enthusiatic student was a spiritual cousin of a young actor I worked with, who was so carried away with the truth that he—on his entrance—threw his hat on the peg of the "fourth" and non-existent wall. It landed on the lap of a lady in the second row who was shocked by the truth but helpfully tossed it back on stage. That was an unexpected diversion in a most dramatic scene.

I think in acting, as in everything else, one has to find one's own center of gravity—to recognize the value and the price of these and like adventures in learning. But more and more I have come to believe that there are only two styles of acting: good and bad.

❈   ❈   ❈

I was in *We Moderns* when Minnie Maddern Fiske was appearing at the Henry Theatre in St. John Ervine's *Mary,*

Mary, Quite Contrary. We played a Wednesday matinee, she a Thursday. I caught a performance and was never to be the same again.

I had never seen such spontaneity of acting. She was a superb comedienne. Mrs. Fiske had a butterfly touch, and she fluttered through the play, barely lighting on the furniture: an ephemeral thing, catching the light, always trembling on the brink of audacity. She was yellow-bright, sunbright. I was dazzled by her.

It was immediately apparent that I was witness to one of those performances of which every actor dreams, and which he may achieve only once in a lifetime. The one we all wait for. The perfect one, where you are lost in your art and can do no wrong. Mrs. Fiske was experiencing this and I was sharing it.

When I left the theatre and the spell was broken, I wondered what she was like without the miracle, without the gods hovering over her. So I bought another ticket and returned on the next Thursday. And the next. And the next. I attended the Henry Miller Theatre for the rest of the season as if it were St. Patrick's Cathedral. Mrs. Fiske became my idol.

To my fascination and, doubtless, the distress of many romantic students, she gave exactly the same performance every single time. There wasn't a smile or a shrug that was a fraction of a second early or late. A crumb was brushed off her jabot at precisely the same moment as she was fashioning a particular syllable. All that incredible spontaneity was calculated to a sigh.

Everything was perfectly synchronized. Whether sitting or standing, or twitching her nose, in sound and movement she was contrapuntal to the melody of the play. She had found the perfect way to convey this delightful character and so her performance was never one jot less than perfect.

Her direct descendent was Ina Claire, who, in comedy, had the same crystalline brightness, the same daisy freshness. Never dark, it was a kind of northern Celtic transparency, if you will, like Waterford crystal.

* * *

Laurette Taylor was all of this when she was young. There is no way of describing the light, the glow of her. When I first became addicted to Laurette, she was winsome and joyous but, unlike Mrs. Fiske, she didn't know (I believe) what wonders she was working and how she worked them. Laurette was tuned in. She transcended technique and even triumphed over her lack of propriety.

Like most geniuses, she could be as dreadful as she could be great. Her taste could be appalling, her stage deportment reprehensible. When she did a performance of *Pierrot* all in mime, which she had never bothered to study, she made no sense whatsoever. She was all stammering hands and adorable bewilderment. And as Juliet, she was absolutely unforgettable. When she did the balcony scene in a special matinee performance and Romeo revealed himself beneath the balcony, our Laurette actually met his eye and whispered, "Hello, Romeo." It was goodbye, Juliet, from that moment on.

Laurette was an arbitrary angel, outrageous, wayward—and to me, at least, adorable.

Like many of our countrywomen, she was not known for her style in dress. I have been notorious for my disinterest in clothes. Elsa Maxwell once remarked that I didn't dress badly; I simply didn't bother to dress at all. And Lynn Fontanne, to this day, sometimes looks at my wardrobe in such exquisite pain that I fear for her. Still, with all of this, I am the Duchess of Windsor and Jacqueline Kennedy combined compared to Laurette Taylor. One cannot describe her get-ups.

The same season that I was doing *To the Ladies* with Otto Kruger, Laurette starred in *National Anthem,* a play written for her by her husband, Hartley Manners. I was able to attend her opening, and I noted in the program that Ethel Frankau, of Bergdorf Goodman, had designed Laurette's wardrobe. She was sitting directly behind me on that first night and I turned to greet her.

"Thank goodness, Ethel, she's in good hands at last," I said.

The designer leaned forward discreetly. "What a time we had with her. But it all worked out just fine. Just wait," she cooed.

When Laurette walked out on the stage in a strange dress of gold cloth, Ethel's voice cut through the loud applause.

"My God," she moaned, "she's got the damn thing on backwards!"

That was our Laurette, bless her—Laurette in her heyday.

When I was in Chicago many years later, playing *Harriet,* she was doing *Glass Menagerie* and, apparently, had won her battle against drink. She was reveling in her enormous success in the Chicago run and the promise of her triumphant return to Broadway. She knew there were so many depending on her—Margot Jones, Eddie Dowling, and a brand-new and very lucky playwright named Tennessee Williams. Laurette was trying—and succeeding. One martini before dinner and a double scotch after the show at her favorite Clark Street restaurant seemed to do the trick. What discipline this required. What a reservoir of strength the theatre demands.

"I'm going to break this witch's curse," she kept saying over and over, like an incantation. And she did—for a while.

When we were strolling down State Street, or wherever, and she saw a liquor store, she would dash off like a thing possessed, with me trying to find her in the crowd. She was that terrified that the mere window display would lure her to her doom.

She was tortured, Laurette was, caught up in her own terrible legend. It was true that in her last years she became helpless, demanding, and intractable. She was lucky to be working at all. Gilbert Miller had fired her from a Henri Bernstein play and, though I was ace-high with him at the time and could have asked for the moon, I couldn't save this dying star. No one would touch her. And then had come *The Glass Menagerie* and the incredible Chicago success, with everyone wondering if she could survive the run and the New York opening.

This was the climate in which she had to work. That she was her own rain-maker makes it no less tragic.

It was one in the morning when I was awakened in Chicago. I could hardly recognize the croaking voice as Laurette's.

"Helen, it's me, I'm sick, sick."

"What's the matter, Laurette?" I asked, certain that I already knew.

"I can't talk. It's my damned voice. How can I play a matinee tomorrow? If I miss that matinee," she whispered threateningly, "they'll say I'm drunk. And if they say I'm drunk, I'll get drunk; and if I get drunk, I'll stay drunk for the rest of my cursed life!"

We got her through that one, and there were hundreds of them until she went on to her last triumph. The last act of her life had as many crises as a revenge play. But I will always cherish memories of my friend Laurette when she was all gaiety and springtime. When she was a sliver of girlish laughter.

> She had a dark and rovin' eye
> And her hair hung down in ringlets

She was a good girl, a decent girl . . .
But one of the roguish kind.

Poor Laurette. Her agonies are over.

* * *

It is vanity to believe that your acting will be touched by the divine more than once or twice. It is realistic to develop your craft so that you can conquer fear and achieve excellence at will, so that your audience will never be disappointed and never be bored.

I suppose everyone must follow his own nose. There are many roads to Rome and there are many guides for those with no sense of direction. Bless them all.

There may be some, like Laurette, who can arrive by magic, over the treetops, soaring. For most, the trip is arduous. I've always done things the hard way: down the dusty road, over the hills, and I get there—once in a while divinely.

During the last week of my tour in *Twelfth Night,* Charlie called from New York, as he did every night. Those telephone calls were both marvelous and depressing—mechanical testimony to the distance between us. Still, on this night, I was ecstatic and screamed, "Charlie, I did it! I did it! I *was* Viola tonight. I found the key!"

Charlie roared with laughter. "May I remind you that you're closing tomorrow night?"

"But Charlie," I explained, "I've got two more whacks at it. Isn't it marvelous?"

And it was. I had been searching for Viola throughout the whole run and captured her at the very last moment. Sometimes it works in reverse. During the long run of a play, it is easy to lose innocence and truth, to become clever. One searches desperately for the original surprise, because without it one is merely performing. This is what I fear I had been doing all those early years. This actor's greatest pitfall has been overconscientiousness, an overweening desire for continuous improvement.

It took me years to learn that the important thing is to convey, as directly and simply as possible, the author's intent —and do it all the time. This will to submerge your personality into another can bring about the most dazzling and spooky results.

One night in Cincinnati the miracle occurred for me. I was playing *Mary of Scotland,* and it had been the dreariest of days—raining, oppressive, heavy. The dampness penetrated the marrow of one's bones. It was like Edinburgh.

I have always loved walking to and from the theatre. Walking is my joy. My head clears before a performance and afterwards it helps me unwind. On this particular evening the company manager, Harry Essex, walked along with me, through the rain, from the hotel. I didn't know how special that night was going to be.

The curtain rose on the performance and I swear a spirit took over. It was terrifying. I was possessed. When Rizzio was murdered, my rage—a queen's rage—was so great that everyone was stunned.

"Douglas, I'll remember this. You pack of filthy cowards!"

My fury transcended everything. It was the way it should always be, but if it were, none of us could survive even one season. I *was* Mary that night.

Actors who usually gossiped backstage between scenes avoided me, for it was a shared experience. Even my dresser was silent. The whole night was awesome. In the last scene in the cell, I returned, defeated by Elizabeth, to my old place in the recessed window, shuddered with the cold of the stone, and stared into the dark future. The curtain came down on deathly silence. Then I heard a fellow actor say, "Gee whiz!" and I was brought back to reality.

It doesn't happen often. It's over-proud to expect it to

happen often. But it's why we actors go on. When it happens, it makes all the fears and failures and disappointments unimportant. All the years of work have added up to that total identification.

When I left the theatre that night, many of the audience were, as always, waiting in the alley. But it was different this night. This had not been a solitary experience. It had been a communion. No one asked for an autograph, no one spoke to me. As I walked out of the stage door with Harry, the crowd separated like the Red Sea. Only as we turned the corner did they break into applause. It was the most sensitive and beautiful tribute. There had been a spell and no one wanted to break it.

An actor's life is spent trying to repeat such moments. I have never gotten over the fact that among some photographs taken by someone in the audience there was one of me in a cape, with my arm extended, in which, I swear, the camera caught the spirit that had possessed me. It is not I, but Mary Stuart, caught in action like some ectoplasmic materialization. There's no explanation. It's just a miracle.

An actor who played with Laurence Olivier in his triumphant *Othello* told me of one performance that transcended all the others. His fellow actors were used to being thrilled by him on stage, but this night they huddled in the wings, uneasy, as if in the presence of real tragedy.

At the end of the play, after his last call—with the audience still cheering—Olivier made his way to his dressing room through two lines of fellow actors who were also applauding him. He ignored them all and slammed the door. When someone knocked and said, "What's the matter, Larry? It was *great!*" the cast heard his voice boom through the door.

"I know it was great, damn it, but I don't know how I did it so how can I be sure I can do it again?"

This is the torture actors go through when they succeed. One can only imagine the humility we feel the rest of the time.

* * *

I have tried hard as an actress in my mature years, and, for all my labors, still have but a handful of moments in which I believe I was touched by God. It doesn't seem enough, after 60 years on stage.

Without the compensation of glamor, I am hard put to explain the durability of my career and the loyalty of the audience. Perhaps it is just identification. I was once the typical daughter, then the easily recognizable wife, and then the quintessential mother. I seem always to have reminded people of someone in their family. Perhaps I am just the triumph of Plain Jane.

My very lack of glamor has kept me a star. I am gratified and shouldn't question my luck, but my own fears and feelings of inadequacy have never wholly left me.

Not only have I retained my sense of wonder, but those of shock and surprise as well. So mysterious are the ways of the Lord that my shortcomings are responsible for my long career.

George Tyler told me that, were I four inches taller, I could become one of the great actresses of my time. That I was so short stuck in my craw, but I decided to lick my size. A string of teachers pulled and stretched till I felt I was in a medieval torture chamber. I gained nary an inch—but my posture became military. I became the tallest five-foot woman in the world. And my refusal to be limited by my limitations enabled me to play Mary of Scotland, the tallest queen in history.

I have used life this way. It is the way it must be used.

9

WHEN Mr. Tyler handed me Carlyle's *The French Revolution* to read, I should have suspected something. He didn't want me to become a Jacobin or —God help him—a libertarian. He simply decided that it was high time that I was personally introduced to the culture of the Continent.

To be properly educated, it was not only necessary to read the best European authors, but to be exposed to the civilizations that cradled them as well. He made all the reservations, all the arrangements, took care of every exigency except one. I had to pay for the trip!

Mother and I quickly got some pencils and paper and determined just how much his generosity was going to cost us. Our mouths hung open.

Two first-class steamship tickets were handed to us. We were to leave on the *Olympic* and we already had our quarters at the Crillon in Paris. When Mother questioned the wisdom of such extravagant accommodations, Mr. Tyler waved her objections away impatiently.

"Helen is a new star. She must be prepared to live like one."

Mother was sorely tempted to quote one of Annie Hess's samplers, "All that glitters is not gold," but she contained herself admirably. Instead, she was reduced, like everyone else in his presence, to wistfulness.

"But we can't afford such a trip, Mr. Tyler—the clothes, the transportation. . . ."

He had an answer for everything. "You can buy the necessary frocks in Paris very cheaply. As for all the other expenses, *I* am spending a fortune on Helen, engaging the very best authors to write for her." He turned to me. "You have got to do your share, my child. The public expects you to live on a grand scale. Your going-away gift will be Eleanor Robson's press book. You will learn, Helen, how a great star lives."

I was soon to learn that Miss Robson, who had become, upon retirement, Mrs. August Belmont, never wore a pair of gloves after the first cleaning. She simply threw them away. Graddy Hayes topped her. She never wore a pair more than once!

Mr. Tyler was no more generous with *Bab* than he had been with *Pollyanna,* so Mother and I had to dig into our small savings. We spent all we had on this trip.

As Mother and I rearranged matters, we sailed through the fanciest lobbies, up the chicest lifts, down the longest red-carpeted corridors to the tiniest of cubbyholes. We shared a broom closet in every smart hotel in Europe.

When the *Olympic* arrived at Cherbourg, Mr. Tyler met us at the dock in a great white open Mercedes, in which his chauffeur Gabriel had driven him from Egypt. The two men were dressed in white dusters and goggles. Mother and I were given white veils and the same accoutrements, which we had to don immediately. I almost died of embarrassment. Waving goodbye to our shipboard friends in these passé get-ups, I could only be grateful it wasn't hello. We were happily and quickly to disappear from their view.

Mr. Tyler had planned everything, down to the smallest detail. He was driving us to his beloved Paris, which I had to approach—like everything else in my life—through his cultivated eyes. I was to be presented with the French countryside, its Boucher foliage and charming little white carts moving through little villages off the beaten tourist track. We would spend the first night in Mont St. Michel, where the famous Madame Poulard would make us one of her famous omelets, and where I would sleep in a featherbed so high that I would have to reach it by ladder. Then we would continue on to Paris, where we would arrive just in time to watch the sun sink behind the *Arc de triomphe*—a sight, I was informed, which had made the freshly gloved Eleanor Robson swoon.

The first time I saw Paris! This man managed to take all the joy out of the most joyous city in the world. Mr. Tyler disapproved of everything that would thrill a young girl.

I adored dancing and he disapproved of the one-step, which was the rage. I adored wandering through the streets and dawdling through museums. With Mr. Tyler we marched. In that introduction to Gallic history, the French Revolution seemed to have lasted ten minutes.

Whether in Paris—at chic luncheons in the Bois and dinners at Maxim's—or in the Loire Valley or at Versailles . . . whether I was tasting *coeur à la crème* and *fraises du bois*, or relishing Fragonards and Ingres . . . I was swallowing France whole, without a chance to savor or digest it.

I would go to bed, exhausted, with my Baedeker, doing

my homework for the next day. I would study our itinerary and read up on the towns we were scheduled to visit. It was pointless. For one so proper, Mr. Tyler had one uncharacteristic outlet: he was a speed demon. He, or Gabriel, at his insistence, would whiz through the countryside, making a blue flash of all the wonderful places I was supposed to be exploring.

I was fascinated by the fact that Gabriel had been secretary, before the war, to the poet Pierre Loti, who had written *Pêcheur d' Islande,* one of the French novels I had studied with Mr. Drew. It was one of the few facts I was able to glean. My European debut was a speedy one—and it could have been so divine.

When Charlie and I traveled through Europe, it was a different story. In my Charlie I found a dallier after my own heart. On my trip with Mr. Tyler, I barely glimpsed the *gorges de Tarn,* those unspoiled limestone plateaus. And when we got to the *château* at Blois, the home of Catherine de Médici and Mary Stuart, I was heartbroken that I couldn't wander through it for days.

Instead, we raced madly over the Louis XV stone bridge, up da Vinci's spiral staircase, through the Francis I and d'Orleans wings. I will never forget that beautiful inn where we stayed in Blois. The full moon spotlighted each of the little tables outside. When we were through dining "Father Barrett" dispatched me to bed, though I wasn't tired, so I would have the strength once again to start cultivating myself, on the double, come dawn.

Mother and Mr. Tyler sat under that French moon loathing each other and testing the local wines, while I was sent off to bed like a child. I lay there listening to *El Relicario* from a nearby cafe. A breeze carried the melody through the open leaded window, billowing the curtains and allowing the moonlight to fill the room with silver. I was in a French inn and the music was so gay. Quite irrationally, I cried myself to sleep.

Our whirling dervish, George Tyler, left us in Paris after two frantic weeks. He also left Freddie Stanhope, his general director, who put on most of his plays, to see that Mother and I got safely to London the following day. There he had arranged for me to meet George Bernard Shaw and Sir James Barrie. He had also engaged a young actor named Leslie Howard to appear with me in the play that Booth Tarkington was writing for me.

The moment Mr. Tyler left Paris, I begged Freddie to take us to the *Folies Bergères* about which I had heard on the ship coming over. I was eager to see the famous Mistinguett, who, according to my shipmates on the *Olympic,* was practically Marianne, La Belle France herself.

Paris ceased being a beautiful prison. Free for the first time in that lovely city, Mother and I were so enchanted with the *Quartier Latin* and Montmartre that I postponed my trip to London for a week.

Those stolen golden days in Paris were to hang like millstones round my neck for years. I had chosen Mistinguett over George Bernard Shaw, frivolity over greatness. I never heard the end of it. Of course, it was part terror. From my earliest celebrity, I have found it painful to consort with the world's great. These meetings almost always end in disaster; I usually mess them up in jig time. I do wish I had a flair. That has always been my greatest flaw.

*   *   *

Our guilty arrival, one week late, at London's Garland Hotel, behind the Haymarket, found us standing in a room filled with dead flowers and that awful funereal scent. It was quite appropriate. I was sure that Mr. Tyler would kill me when he discovered my recalcitrance. I almost saved him the trouble when I read the stack of notes left at the desk.

In my childish quest for pleasure in Paris, I had neglected some of the most important people in England. Mr. Tyler had asked them to look me up and had arranged all sorts of social engagements for me. Now I couldn't look anyone in London straight in the eye.

A postcard with a picture of Rodin's *Balzac* attracted my attention. When I gingerly turned it over, I read, "Sorry I couldn't wait your visit any longer. G.B.S." It was dated the day before, from the Isle of Man. I fell into a chair in shock. It was outrageous. I had played hookey from history. I had failed Mr. Tyler and myself.

An even greater disappointment was a note from Sir James Barrie's secretary. He was off to Scotland and "terribly disappointed," though he sent me a white kid-bound copy of *Peter Pan* and a set of his plays. I hated myself for a couple of days. But Leslie Howard fixed all that by showing me his London from the top of the red double-deckers instead of a white Mercedes. Mother and I felt cozy and at home, remembering our early New York days. He took us to little theatrical restaurants and wangled free seats for us for many of the West End hits. No wonder that after such an introduction London remains my favorite city. Conversely Paris fills me with melancholy, and I always race through it.

One afternoon, from the window of my hotel, I did spy Sir James Barrie, pensively walking along the Mews. He was bizarre, with a large, bulging forehead like Baudelaire's that melted down to a little pointed chin. He was alone and deep in thought and it was rewarding for me to see him this way, a writer in thought and not on display. That's as near as I ever got to him after my tardy arrival.

I was, however, given a second chance with Bernard Shaw

some years later, when we met at Lady Throckmorton's at Coughton Court, Warwickshire. The stately home was built for Lord Francis Throckmorton by Elizabeth I. He had been her ambassador to Mary Stuart. Since the Gunpowder Plot was hatched there, the ensuing explosion resulted in a cloud over the family. The Crown reduced the family title to a simple baronetcy.

The Dowager Lady Throckmorton, whose charming but drowsy son Sir Robert was dubbed The Sleepy Baronet by Charlie, had a pleasant exchange with the then 80-year-old playwright, who was not in the best of moods. For the first time in his life, he was about to have a tooth pulled and he was furious.

Shaw was a testy Irish terrier—spirited and spry—a grizzled, ancient puppy of a man with a complexion so beautiful that it was remarkable. Mary Anderson, herself an octogenarian, who, I believe, had been painted as Juliet by Rossetti, remarked about it with an envy all the ladies present shared.

"Now, Bernard," she teased, "I don't want to hear any canard about splashing your face with icewater and rubbing it off with the sleeve of your Norfolk jacket. You don't have a line or a wrinkle. What is the secret?"

"Comfortable boots and open bowels," he snapped, putting an end to her.

As for me, he had remembered the unfortunate incident that took place years before. Perhaps too well. We were all to suffer that day from his fear of dentistry, and consequently not to be spared his bite.

"You're appearing in Housman's *Victoria,* aren't you?" he asked amiably enough.

"Yes, Mr. Shaw," I replied. Laurence Housman had told me that G.B.S. was mad about his play.

"Silly little part, isn't it?" Shaw now observed, dispensing with the zenith of both the British Empire and my career in one fell swoop.

*   *   *

Mr. Tyler was really trying to build that career in those early years. He tried desperately. Despite my inability to shine offstage, he never stopped treating me like a star.

I had first met Booth Tarkington through him. On my return to America after that first trip to the Continent, he had arranged a week for me in Kennebunkport at the Tarkingtons' house to discuss *The Wren,* which the author was finishing for me.

Throughout this period of grooming and work, Mr. Tyler also commissioned the wildly successful Marc Connelly and George S. Kaufman to write me a vehicle. It turned out to be *To the Ladies.* I was a fortunate girl. Young actresses today simply do not have this kind of help.

Years later, when I was firmly established, I spoke to Lawrence Langner about brilliant actresses like Julie Harris and Kim Stanley, Anne Bancroft and Susan Strasberg. Why were they not kept working, their careers given continuity? Why didn't the Guild Theater, with its power, protect them and groom them for enduring stardom?

Nothing is quite as simple as his explanation, but it is true that the long-term contracts the old producers made an actor sign are no longer allowed. Out of the tyranny and excesses of such producers as Belasco and Tyler came Actors Equity. But there is a price for the greater freedom the performer now enjoys. I was a Tyler slave, his chattel, his property, but I was protected and I flourished.

I remember one season when Mother and I were really desperate. We had spent all our savings on a trip to Italy with Mr. Tyler, and there was no play ready for me when we returned. Mr. Tyler insisted that I await the right script.

There were glamorous and vague plans, but there was nothing definite and we were out of funds. Other managements such as William Brady and George M. Cohan were eager to employ me, but the mere hint of such a reasonable alternative to starvation sent my mentor into long diatribes on loyalty. Though we had no written contract and I was now in demand, his word was still Athenian law. His grasp of economics was also patrician. He lived in such a rarified world. When Mother asked him how we were supposed to survive, his answer was swift and to the point.

"Don't you have any friends you can visit?"

It was just this kind of regal attitude that brought about the actor's revolution and the formation of Actors Equity Association.

Mr. Tyler's flat insistence that I not join the union was alienating me from all my friends—like Humphrey Bogart, Helen Mencken, Kenneth MacKenna, and Margalo Gilmore. Frank Gilmore, Margalo's father, was the first president of Equity, and it was clear to all but the blind that the Fidelity League—not so affectionately known as the Fidoes and made up mostly of producers and powerful stars—would lose out to the inevitable.

Everyone I knew importuned me to join them in a strong Equity Association—Ethel Barrymore, Mary Boland, everyone. It seemed that virtually only the producers were sympathetic to the Fidoes. The day of the martinet producer was seeing its sunset. Both his tyranny and royal patronage were over. Both the good and the bad.

Under Mr. Tyler's domination I attended Fido meetings and listened to Mr. William Collier, Mrs. Fiske, and Mr. George M. Cohan as they—all of them—spoke of protecting the status quo, thereby consolidating their powerful positions. I felt like a traitor to my peers and just couldn't live with myself.

My chums weren't angry but they were all disappointed
that I couldn't stand up to Mr. Tyler. But I hadn't been
encouraged to stand up to anyone in my life. It was an impasse until John Halliday took me to lunch one day. He
begged me to defy Tyler and join the other young actors.

"You belong with your family, Helen—the other kids who
are struggling—"

I thought of Pat Neaves and the whole string of unpro-
tected girls who lived so precariously on Broadway and on
tours—always subject to the whims of an often unfeeling
management.

"Oh, I want to, Jack—but Mr. Tyler would never let me."

"Then do it anyway."

"But he's been so wonderful to me."

Then Jack Halliday told me that George Cohan had
wanted me for a play called *In Love With Love* and had
asked Mr. Tyler to allow me to appear opposite Jack. Though
Mr. Tyler had no other work for me, he refused—not even
telling me of the offer. Lynn Fontanne had been given the
role.

"I hardly think you have to worry about loyalty after
that," Jack said. "And anyway, Tyler will accept the fact,
once it is accomplished. Believe me, Helen—you have nothing to worry about—you've *got* to be with us."

I was certainly startled by this bit of news. It seemed unbelievable that Mr. Tyler could be so proprietary when he
knew how desperate I was for work. But it was just one more
symptom of the power Equity was fighting.

By the time lunch was over, Jack had given me the
strength to follow my instinct.

Mother agreed with me completely but waited outside the
Tyler office when I gritted my teeth and went in to see him.
Mother felt that, since he found her so abrasive, her presence
could only further enrage him. But I don't believe he could

have been more coldly furious. Mr. Tyler simply looked down at some papers on his desk.

"If you walk out of this office," he said, "there is no turning back."

I walked out.

Mr. Tyler's despotism had a great deal of benevolence. He was from another time and, like his goggles and duster, his scrapbooks of Eleanor Robson, he was—in the 1920's—an anachronism, like the last pronunciamento of an exiled king. But along with his outdated pomposity and *noblesse oblige,* he trailed a courtliness and a refinement of taste plus a commitment to the theatre and to me for which I will always be grateful.

He was a 19th-century gentleman and he lost me to the 20th. Before he dismissed me, he had made me one of the leading young stars in New York. It was a painful separation, but George C. Tyler had done such a good job that my career could now soar without him.

10

I DIDN'T feel much like a star the day I met Charlie at Neysa McMein's studio on 57th Street. Marc Connelly had seen me on Fifth Avenue, and after I agreed to help him choose a gift for Margalo Gilmore, I unwillingly allowed him to drag me to one of the few legitimate salons in New York. I was starring in his play *To the Ladies*, but knew few celebrities other than those with whom I might have been working. My friends were still to become famous and it was still possible to feel at ease with them.

Miss McMein's studio overwhelmed me, and so did she. Our hostess sat on a raised platform in a smock and beret, a warm and untidy person with tawny hair and a lazy, purring manner. She was like a tortoise-shell cat who had attended art school. She managed for years to retain the expectant quality of a young artist—about to arrive, on the threshold, always at the beginning. When I met her that afternoon, she sat before her easel working on a new cover for *Cosmopolitan Magazine,* ostensibly unaware of her glittering guests.

The large room fairly crawled with celebrity. Marc, as the latest arrival, took center stage, greeting one and all with a heartiness and enthusiasm that would never have suggested that he had seen everyone of these people the evening before.

Between four and seven every day, Miss McMein's marvelous sky-lighted studio was a must for the town's bright new talents. They were attracted like bees to honey and the constant buzz was of sweet success.

My entrance was not particularly hailed, and, after a few perfunctory introductions, I found a corner and sat drinking it all in. Slim, dark Irving Berlin was at the piano, resembling one of the black notes, and the exotic, prognathous George Gershwin was straining at the leash to replace him. Robert Benchley, an enchanted toad of a man, was croaking with laughter at a new joke Marc had just whispered to him, and the patrician Alice Duer Miller was monopolizing my idol of the moment, Shaw's *St. Joan*—the wonderful actress Winifred Lenihan. *To the Ladies'* co-author, George S. Kaufman, and his wife, Beatrice, carved for each other like primitive sculptures, dominated a large group of admirers; and the waspish Alexander Woollcott was, for the moment, smiling benignly, presiding over the honeycomb as if it were the Seventh Day and he had created it all and couldn't have been more pleased with the results.

I sipped my ginger ale and devoured the whole scene. It would have been the most exciting in my life, had I not been so painfully a part of it.

It was a stage set, and the most trivial utterance emerged as polished dialogue. No one ever just *said* anything there. Everyone was *on*—shining and outshining. I sat terrified that I would be asked the time of day and have to coin a *bon mot* in reply. This was not a room in which one could ever simply say "Six twenty." What a bore! I suppose "Everything is at sixes and sevens" might have given me high marks, but it has taken me 35 years to think of it and this crowd was a fast one and not in a waiting mood.

Since they were virtually all famous strangers to me, their gossip was way over my head. Snatches of conversations, tag lines of stories, esoteric references to soubriquetted friends would create a swell of uproarious mirth that was shared by all—except me. For fear that I might be thought a simpleton or stone-deaf or possibly both, I would occasionally cock my head with knowing amusement or lower my eyelids in tolerant acceptance of the madness that prompted Dotty to say, "Really!" with such pith or provoked Harpo to insist, "You're slightly, Dotty!"

I didn't know what in tarnation anybody was talking about. Durable Irving—still at the piano—was playing his *Always* with one finger, like a little boy, and that lovely melody drifted toward me over the din along with the most beautiful young man I'd ever seen. He stood looking down at me with hazel eyes dabbed with green. His hair was curly, his ears pointed. This was a mouth designed exclusively for smiling. He looked exactly like a faun, though Brownie later informed me that from what she heard—and it was the most reliable of sources—he was worse; he was a "satire!"

"Do you want a peanut?" this enchanting creature asked.

My Charlie's life was composed almost entirely of brilliant curtain lines. Openers or closers, the *mot juste,* the phrase that would tie up a situation always outlived the crisis that inspired it. He was a writer, and his gift was regretted only once in his whole life. In his never-ending compulsion to live up to his legend he now found it necessary to invent a phrase that unfortunately proved deathless.

It wasn't enough that he poured the peanuts from a

crumpled paper bag into my trembling hands. He had to add, "I wish they were emeralds."

Of course, I was bowled over. Starting with Mother, that evening, I told everyone who would listen all about it. When in Hollywood some years later, I wanted to be cooperative with an interviewer and I repeated it again, the line was committed to print. From that moment on, it was to haunt us. Even as late as our tenth anniversary, which we celebrated *à deux* at his favorite bistro, "21," we found a bowl of dyed-green peanuts awaiting us on our table, the artwork of the owners—the famous Jack and Charlie. Such antics over the years so depressed Charlie that, at the end of World War II, returning from India and the Eastern Theater, he dumped a bag of emeralds in my lap.

"I wish they were peanuts," was his only comment.

Charlie MacArthur! Playwright and playboy, reporter and soldier of fortune, blazing wit and the eternal, white-haired boy—my Charlie.

It is a miracle that he rescued me from the corner of that studio and from the shadows of an endless childhood. He saw the woman lurking in the girl. It was Charlie who gave my life reality, who handed me my sovereignty, the identity that completed my education as an actress and began it as a woman.

I didn't believe my good luck the day of Neysa's party. The catch of all time had singled me out and taken me home in a hansom cab, spouting outrageous nonsense to any passerby who happened to catch his eye. Workmen tearing up the street with pneumatic drills brought forth the solicitous query, "Lose a nickel, Buddies?" A bunch of office workers rushing out of a building on their way home gave him as we sat in his carriage, a sense of regality. With a langorous wave of his hand in their direction, he cried aloud to all Park Avenue, "Let them eat cake!"

He dropped me at 15 Park Avenue with a promise to call. It was just too good to be true.

I waited for days, for weeks and he never got in touch with me. I felt like Madame Butterfly. Having filled Mother's ears with nothing but "Charlie MacArthur, Charlie MacArthur," I was now told that it was just as well, that my work was more important than any man. Mother was sure that he was another of the boys who had appeared and then vanished at her displeasure.

"Maybe he doesn't know how to reach you," Jean Dixon tried valiantly.

To the Ladies had closed and I was now playing in *Quarantine* with Sidney Blackmer and the redoubtable Kay Laurell. Anyone who could read a newspaper, no less write one, knew that.

"Maybe he's taken the title seriously," I bantered. But there was no laughter in my heart. I was filled with nothing but Charlie MacArthur. I was smitten mightily.

Sometimes life does imitate art; the convergence of events at this point suggests a playwright at work. The 24-year-old wren, Miss Prissy Prune, the girl Charlie MacArthur hadn't called, was wanted by the Theater Guild to play Shaw's *Cleopatra,* the part I had coveted since my Sacred Heart days. I had even written my term paper on that play, scandalizing the Sisters. I had dreamed of playing her. Some dreams do come true, I thought. The Guild's new theatre was being completed; President Coolidge was to press a button at the White House, officially opening this most distinguished of seasons.

For the first time, I interfered with Mother's interference in negotiating the contract. We had come far in the theatre and Mother had gained confidence. It was true that the Guild was not notorious for its princely salaries, but when Mother hung up on Theresa Helburn in regal disdain after

hearing the offer—imagine! she just put down the receiver!—
I left the house and called the lady from the corner drugstore.

Nobody was going to stop me from playing *Cleopatra,* not
even Brownie. There were doubts on Broadway that my
sheltered life and obvious innocence qualified me for the
role of the feline young queen, but I was an awakening fe-
male and, by this time, I was an actress. It was difficult to
cross Mother, but I *had* to play that part.

I won't deny that underlying the all-consuming work that
went into the preparation of the role, I had the romantic
notion that my Mark Anthony might be inspired to pick up
a telephone, but it would have been an anachronism.

Every single night of that run, I stood like a fool looking
through the peephole of the curtain to see if, by some miracle, Charlie were there. He had simply disappeared into thin
air.

Helen Westley, our Fatateetah and one of the Guild's
board of directors, chastised me for counting the house. Miss
Westley thought it was unseemly that so young a star should
reveal herself so mercenary. It is true that Bernhardt used
to demand her salary in gold ducats which she counted and
then carried off in bags, but her age and legend gave her
that privilege.

"My dear," her metallic voice squeaked, "concern yourself
with your part. Let the box-office people—"

"I'm not counting the house, Helen!" I interrupted. "I'm
looking for someone."

Helen arranged her red flannel underwear under her costume. She wore flannels because we all had colds from this
dampest of stages. Virtually unfinished backstage, the brand-
new theatre was dank with still-wet plaster. Our makeup
would run and saturate us; then the draughts would get us.
As Cleopatra, I wore little. As my nurse, the older actress—

as casual a performer as I ever worked with—would hide her long johns with only occasional success. Almost nightly, a red leg or sleeve would fall. Utterly undisturbed, she would push it back, not missing a beat. She'd been through it all— a real veteran.

"Someone special?" she asked, raising her wonderfully hooded grey eyes, simultaneously dropping the purple bags beneath them.

"Uhumm!" I admitted.

"Does he come every night? How *marvelous!*"

"He hasn't come at all."

"Why don't you send him a ticket?"

"No! Oh, no!" I fairly shouted.

"Why don't you call him?"

"Oh, I couldn't."

"If *I'm* after a man I call him up until he moves."

"I'll wait," I answered. "He'll come."

Finally, one Saturday night my dresser announced, "There's a Mr. MacArthur to see you." He hadn't seen the performance but was simply passing the theatre and saw my picture out front.

Aline Bernstein had designed the flimsiest of black chiffon costumes for the last scene, and Charlie now stood in my dressing room, just staring at its bodice. I had never been more visible nor more transparent.

"Would you have supper with me?" he asked, watching my heart.

"I can't," I gasped. "I have to go home to Syosset, Long Island. We've borrowed a house for the season. It's a long drive—" I trailed off.

There was silence. His famous, roving eye hadn't roved an inch.

"Perhaps you'd like to come to Syosset and have supper

there," I now heard myself say. "You can pick up some things and stay the weekend with us."

"I don't need anything," he answered.

Halcyon Hargrove—one of my Washington school friends in the cast, who was eventually to marry the music critic James Wittaker—drove us to Syosset to the handsome house Paul Hammond had lent us. Presently grouse-hunting in Scotland, our old friend had even left us his Japanese houseboy. I felt Charlie would be impressed. I wanted so to impress him.

Mother and my other house guest, June Walker, were awaiting us with mixed interest. I had called them. June's heart was all pitter-pat; Mother's was thumping. She had thought Charlie was out of the picture. But after that weekend, he was never to be out of it again.

❊ ❊ ❊

Starting with the summer circuit and treks to Mamaroneck to Neysa McMein and her husband Jack Baragwanath, and to Port Washington to the Herbert Bayard Swopes', and to Great Neck to Tommy Hitchcock's—a summer filled with treasure hunts and swimming and mint juleps and games galore—I tagged along with my Charlie entering the world he loved so much and for which I felt totally unequipped.

In the midst of my love, waves of loathing would come over me for this most divine of men. He had lured me out of the safe corner of my world and was exposing me to the keen and devastating eye of a cyclone. The big wind was Alexander Woollcott, the New York *Herald* drama critic, the Town Crier, the self-styled arbiter of protocol. He was always either bedazzled or contemptuous. There was nothing in between. He believed he was the center of the universe and that, since he was the sun, everything and everybody revolved around him. They did. It was mass hypnosis, I suppose.

A cosmic sport, Alex had somehow managed to create this universe by employing his superiors as satellites. I clearly remember walking home from a Nyack movie with Thornton Wilder, who bitterly confessed his resentment of this inequitable consignment.

"I know I'm better than that whole Algonquin crowd, but I can't act it when I'm with them."

How intimidating they could be. Charlie told me that he always stayed until the end of a party, fearful to leave even two of these friends to make mincemeat of him. That divine circle could be so corrupting and so destructive. The smallest infraction could result in lacerating ridicule.

But I was to learn that Charlie, the most shimmering of that heaven's ornaments, often gravitated toward self-destruction. I saw none of this then. I only knew that in this brilliant assembly of deities, I was being shown up as only too mortal.

            ❄   ❄   ❄

One of the first parties Charlie took me to in town was at Harold Ross's. He was soon to launch *The New Yorker* magazine, and he was Woollcott's closest chum. In honor of the occasion, Alec had invented a new drink of brandy and heavy sweet cream, naming it Alexander after, of course, himself. And well named it was—being both lethal and oversweet, the two extremes he most enjoyed. The drinks seemed innocuous; I had two.

"Everybody," as they say, was there. Chinchilla-ed Jeanne Eagles, carrying her own magnums of champagne; Madeleine and Ernest Boyd; Jascha Heifetz; Lawrence Stallings, fresh from his great success, *What Price Glory?*; crumpled and St. Bernardish Heywood Broun, of whom it was said that he had someone wear his new suits for a couple of years before he would put them on; the famous diagnostician Franklin Pierce Adams, who had announced—when I appeared in *The Wren*—that I was suffering from "fallen archness"; Irving Berlin and George Gershwin, still vying for the piano; Alfred Lunt and his Lynn; Alice Duer Miller; Paul Robeson; Harpo Marx—everybody. They swirled around me, all of them so bright, all of them so witty.

Those Alexanders, which I thought tasted like a Huyler's soda, were getting to me. *I have to say something*, I decided, as the room went round. *I want Charlie to be proud of me. I can't sit here like a frog on a leaf.*

When Kaufman and Connelly wrote *To The Ladies* for me, they asked if I could play the piano. "Of course," I had lied. Mother and I quickly bought a miniature grand and I learned enough to pass muster. The play had come and gone and we were moving to a smaller apartment with a more chic address—another stylish cubbyhole. We had no room for the piano.

There was one of those pauses at the Ross party where everyone stops talking as if on cue. My voice came loud and clear. Frances Robinson Duff had done her work well.

"Anyone who wants my piano," I said sweetly, "is willing to it."

George Kaufman broke the silence.

"That's very seldom of you, Helen," he answered.

I retired to my corner, only to be dragged out to play some alphabet game at which everyone else shone. My God, they loved games. It was their life. I got the booby prize that night. Alice Miller was kind enough to say that I lost because, unlike the rest of the group, I was incapable of using profanity. This, supposedly, made me the dullest of four-letter words—a lady.

No matter which party, it was always the same. Helen

landed on her face and it didn't seem to bother Charlie at all. He never even seemed to notice.

I remember one Christmas at Neysa's. Everyone was sparkling again, and again I decided to assert myself my own way. I started to pass around a ten-pound box of candy and, of course, I dropped it. The guests fell to their hands and knees—all except me. I was incapable of anything more than sinking into the nearest seat. With appetites stimulated by all this exercise, everyone rose as dinner was announced. That darling George Gershwin, who had been sitting with me, now held my arm, and, in a confiding tone, bade me wait a moment. After those near us had left, he pulled out his handkerchief. It seems I had sat on a couple of chocolate creams.

He de-candied me, but the ivory moire sofa was hopeless. I wanted to die, but after a furtive look around, George turned the seat cushion over, fluffed it and then extended his arm elegantly to escort me into the dining room.

Charlie seemed always to ignore these lapses, and I slowly gained confidence through him. It is remarkable that this whole group eventually not only accepted me as Charlie's girl, but became my devoted friends as well. They really came to care for me. This puzzling acceptance became clear to me later on in life. Egocentrics are attracted to the inept. It gives them one more excuse for patting themselves on the back.

I thank heavens that I closed my ears to all the Cassandras who worried about me and heralded our doom. No one in New York approved of Charlie for me. All that mattered was that I had waited patiently for my feller and he had arrived. Of that I was certain. There was the usual price for such happiness as I knew as Charlie's wife, and I paid it.

Our life was crammed with abyssmal moments and glorious hours. I can only say that, were it possible to bear once more the burden of joy and grief I knew as Mrs. Charles MacArthur, I would square my shoulders and welcome the encore.

> I knew my love by his way of talking
> I knew my love by his way of walking. . . .

Charlie once said, "Helen—I may never be able to give you contentment but you'll never be bored."

Happy the one who recognizes one's fate and accepts it.

11

NEYSA McMEIN was terribly concerned because Charlie and Beatrice Lillie were in the midst of a romance and she felt I was a summer replacement. "When Bea gets back from England," she shrugged, "you'll be out in the cold."

Alice Duer Miller was next. "You're out of your depth— Lady Jane Grey in the royal henhouse. Steel yourself for the tenth day."

Charlie's roommate, Bob Benchley, was torn between loyalty and pity. "You're one of the marrying kind. You want to live with Mercury? Just try putting bedroom slippers on those winged feet."

Woollcott, who worshiped Charlie and adored the intrigue even more, now informed Rebecca of Sunnybrook Farm that she would never survive, that even the self-possessed Dorothy Parker had been driven to despair and near-suicide by this most eloquent satyr.

"One might say she was at her wit's end," Alec added, rolling the after-thought around in his mouth like a bon bon.

Harpo Marx pulled up the corners of his mouth. "Do you want to think up a plot and a backer for a movie starring Valentino and Baby Peggy?"

"It's a plain case of mis-casting," George Kaufman agreed.

"He's really interested in *me*," confided the adorable June Walker.

"He's unsteady. . . ."

"He's a lecher. . . ."

"He's a rake. . . ."

"He's a cad and a bounder. . . ."

"He's got a wife in Chicago. . . ."

"He's insane, I tell you. He set fire to Colonel Roosevelt on Fifth Avenue. . . ."

"He'll destroy you. . . ."

It was a barrage, and when the rat-tat-tat stopped, Mother joined the army.

"He *drinks*," she said darkly.

*　*　*

Charlie MacArthur was the son of an evangelist—another one with a private line to God. His father was William Telfer MacArthur, a first-generation American whose parents came from Aberdeen, Scotland. One day on his Pennsylvania farm, he watched his threshing machine go up in flames and, midst the crackle and the orange glow, he stood transfixed. He had heard the call.

A self-propelling man, he not only answered it, but he ordained himself a minister right then and there. The rest of his life was spent chasing fires—the fires of hell and damnation in the souls of men. He made his way across to Chicago and back East, and then down the Hudson, screaming "Repent!" all the way to Nyack, where he settled, using halls and fields as tabernacles for his followers before he joined the Missionary Institute.

He could smell a sinner five miles away on a windless day. Charlie's Bible-ridden, sin-sniffing father would have got along famously with Patrick Hayes. They had much in common. They both had hard-working, fun-loving, antic wives who had to bear the burden of their sanctimony and improvidence, and they both bred children who rebelled against their faith.

Charlie was seven years old when he developed a boil on his neck. His beloved mother, Georgianna, with nine children and plenty of experience, was ready to make a poultice of linseed oil and an old woolen sock. But the deacon was wild-eyed with the discovery of Beelzebub's interest in his son.

The boil was an eruption from the underworld and only prayer would release the pressure. The boy was filled with sin, and this affliction was his punishment.

For one solid week, young Charlie sat beneath naptha lights on a platform, to be watched and prayed over by the reverend's following. Unable to straighten his neck because the carbuncle was so large, the child sat hang-dog, as the chanting went on and the lights grew hissingly hotter. On the seventh night, God heard the deacon's prayers and the miracle occurred.

The sweating boy felt wetter and stickier as the boil burst open and ran down his slim little neck. The rejoicing and hosannas could be heard far and wide. Charlie was brought home in a triumph of faith over matter.

Charlie was schooled at Wilson Academy, which trained missionaries and was staffed by men who considered all joy a sin. There was no dancing, no movies, no unmonitored reading, and no fraternizing with the hedonistic, pagan students of the Nyack high school.

The MacArthur house was filled at mealtime with the itinerant faithful, who stayed for supper, though his mother could barely feed her brood of nine. One cabbage would be stretched to fill 25 mouths. When her husband would cavalierly announce 12 extra for Sunday dinner, Charlie's mother would simply add water to the lemonade, but her sense of humor led her to mute comment. She served the drink to her uninvited guests from the chamberpot, "the only vessel big enough to hold the libation."

She did everything to get rid of these hungry believers, and kept reducing their portions until she was serving them empty plates. To no avail. She was astonished that they were actually thriving on prayer alone, though the reverend considered it simply the just reward of the devout. Mrs. MacArthur had her doubts, which were substantiated when she found food hidden under their clothes and in their packs.

As Charlie said, "We had some elbow room in the house after that."

Old man MacArthur was on a never-ceasing search for wickedness, not only abroad but at home as well. Charlie told me that he and the other boys would be stood against the wall at night for any infraction, like suspects in a police line-up. A strap soaked in vinegar was always ready to use in the service of the Lord, and the boys would have their shirts removed and be whipped, while their father, eyes shining, implored God to forgive not him, but his children.

With all their poverty and all that prayer, it was inevitable that the MacArthur boys—Telfer, Alfred, and John—after their mother's early death from exhaustion, should all become multimillionaires, and Charlie a wild one.

He got as far away as possible when he joined General Pershing on his search for Pancho Villa down Mexico way, and next enlisted in the Rainbow Division in World War I, bringing both great honor and greater hangovers on himself. When the war was over, he returned to Chicago and landed as a reporter for the famous *Examiner*, where he met Ben Hecht and lived the experiences under Walter Howey's editorship that inspired their wonderful play, *Front Page*.

Charlie ran from all that was stuffy and sacrosanct and self-righteous. As Mother had done with her own father, Charlie simply turned his face away from organized religion.

I came to know Reverend MacArthur myself and do not have to trust the subjective eye of a son. He was still perfectly cast as an itinerant preacher when I met him. He was tall and gaunt and white-bearded—a road-company Jehovah. By that time, his loyal and successful sons were seeing to it that he could continue his life of dedication without starving.

He refused to come to see me in the theatre, which he considered a cesspool of vice. Charlie lured him through the stage door once and my father-in-law caught sight of me on a stage.

"You are a sinner," he announced, pointing his bony finger at me when I made my exit.

But the old man mellowed, and, before his Bible was closed for the last time, I had been forgiven my life's work and become first his "dear daughter-in-law" and then his "dear, darling daughter."

*   *   *

My father-in-law, with his tardy but infinite mercy, had forgiven me; but I had a higher judge to concern myself with. Helen Hayes Brown, the devout little Catholic girl who once dreamed of being a nun, who—in discord with her own mother's disbelief—attended church regularly, was now in love with a married man. And a Protestant!

At no time did I consider any alternative to marrying Charlie. But wedding a divorced man meant instant excommunication for me.

It is both terrible and marvelous to admit that I was not given the slightest pause. The strait-laced girl who at 24 was out of another era, at 25 was a woman in love. I was ready to rebel against Mother and Mother Church. To me, it was an offense against God to come between two people in love.

In my arrogance, I would have stood up to the Holy Father himself.

I fed my righteous fury with the Establishment by remembering how the poorest parishioners—the charwomen and trolley conductors at St. Patrick's Cathedral—were pushed to the back and never had seats. How they hovered in the background and then practically genuflected when the Papal Count John McCormick would strut down the aisle in a parade of arrogance, accompanied by what one could almost hear as a drum roll and the blasts of Gabriel's horn.

If you want to find a flaw, you can find one. And I was looking. The excesses of any religion are not its substance, however. I was proud and angry that the Church was disapproving of my love. All the willful and rebellious Irish awakened in me to fight to preserve it and I was going to nit-pick if I so chose.

Our courtship was a long and rough one, and the forces against it were attacking from all directions. I could—at the risk of eternal damnation—ignore the warnings from Rome, but I had to render unto Caesar what was Caesar's. I could marry a divorced man, but I couldn't by law marry a married one.

Charlie's wife had begun her divorce proceedings against him long before I ever came along; but his present willing-

ness to grant her freedom and his growing fame now discouraged her from accepting it. They had been separated for
years, and she was perfectly willing to live without Charlie;
it was the name Mrs. MacArthur she was loath to relinquish.

It was a long, unpleasant business, but, after much counterpoint and many counter-suits, Carol in defeat announced
to the press that she "wouldn't have Charlie MacArthur if
he came in a box of Cracker Jack."

I would and I did. He was my prize, and now that it was
possible legally, I refused to allow anything to keep us apart
any longer.

* * *

While I was playing *What Every Woman Knows*, Charlie
gave me an engagement ring from Cartier's. I wore it on a
chain around my neck, in this most public of secret romances.
At this point, Mother bought me a band of rubies and
emeralds.

I was more bothered by my Church's stand than I admitted, and Father Hurney, my confessor in Washington,
warned me that it would be very difficult to live without the
Church.

"I will never regret it," I said stoutly. And I never really
have.

It seemed wrong for there to be one blanket rule that
covered such a variety of people with such a variety of
problems. With all the pride of youth and all the strength
of one freshly in love, I scorned all those who would keep
me from my man. I was smarter than my mother, smarter
than the Pope.

Sensitive iconoclast that he was, Charlie was distressed by
the position I was forced into. He offered to have his first
marriage declared illegal so I need not be spiritually exiled.

He had been married by his father and, through some fancy footwork, he could save me from sinning in the eyes of the Church.

I wouldn't hear of it. Declaring Reverend MacArthur's ceremony invalid would have stripped the old man's waning life of all meaning. Mother didn't like crutches and neither did I.

"You are not going to say that your father's words weren't sanctified in heaven," I declared.

Not certain I would be welcome up there any longer, I now set the date, with the inner assurance that Jesus would be more tolerant than His vicar on earth.

The obstacles, however, were not all swept away. There was one last hurdle.

❋　❋　❋

Mother's objections were not religious and they were not subtle.

"You're making a fatal mistake," she started.

"I love him, Mother."

"*Love!* What about your career? The first thing you know, you'll have children."

"No, Mother, we're going to wait."

"Wait? Ha!" she exploded triumphantly. "That's what I said when I married Frank Brown—and look what happened to me."

We stood just staring at each other in embarrassment. To my mother, Charlie was a plagiarist. He was going to sign his name to her creation. More and more, I was deferring to him and, more and more, through Charlie I was gaining confidence. Even the unhappy challenge of his cronies was smoothing my rough edges. I was to discover that I really wasn't a dunce at all and I was making friends—Charlie's friends. What I only intuitively knew then was that, unlike Brownie, Charlie wanted me to be strong, and was determined to strengthen further what he was attracted to.

"He'll ruin your life, that 'satire,'" Mother went on. "He'll leave you for another woman, mark my words. Clap hands, here comes Charlie! Ha! A little trouble and poof! There goes Charlie."

Beatrice Lillie had not been a problem at all. When she had first returned from England, bringing Charlie a Sulka robe, he refused it as too expensive a gift. He explained the situation and introduced us.

With all the grace and delicacy so evident in her comic genius, she arrived at Alice Duer Miller's at Christmas with a little dime-store China dog for her ex-beau. Around its neck a cord hung which asked, "Is this a proper gift?"

I can still see her shining eyes, her crescent nose, those braids around her ears. I was lucky to gain in her a life-long friend.

* * *

Others were not so generous to this stranger who was usurping everybody's favorite—the extra man, the perfect catalyst. Charlie was going to be taken out of circulation, and that awful little Helen was responsible. The un-pin-down-able, rocketing Charlie would probably become a crashing bore with his serious, prissy little wife.

"She's a monster!" decided Ethel Barrymore, in stentorian tones. My good friend Alexander Woollcott reported this to me with relish.

He was so adored, Charlie, so treasured, and he was so burdened with this adoration. Socialites and bohemians, everyone everywhere, saw him coming and knew there would be "lively doings." Many of these were sleepyheads

CULVER PICTURES

Helen Hayes Brown

The Charlie who
walked into my life

We were on our way

We were so happy

With Father and Mary

It was Mother's birthday and Charlie took us to the Stork Club

With Lew Fields
and his daughter Dorothy
in Hollywood

Victoria at home with Mary and Jamie

Mary was so lovely

Reverend MacArthur and Jamie, his irreverent grandson

Colonel MacArthur,
our children, and the
mad Camille

Mary made her debut with me in *Alice Sit by the Fire*

Charlie and I on Ed Murrow's "Person-to-Person"

Jim and his Charlie, my grandson

With Joyce and her Mary, my granddaughter

I guess I'm just not serious enough

With Jesse Glendenning in
The Prodigal Husband

Old Dutch

With Lew Fields' Company
in 1910

With John Drew in *The Prodigal Husband*

Coquette

With Clark Gable in *White Sister*

With Gary Cooper in *Farewell To Arms*

WHITE STUDIOS

With William Gillette in *Dear Brutus*

Mary, Queen of Scots

The Young Victoria

Victoria Regina, Empress of India

Harriet Beecher Stowe

Twelfth Night   *Mrs. McThing*

Signora Frola in *Right You Are*   Mrs. Fisher in *The Show Off*

At the Mary MacArthur Memorial Fund Dinner

who needed to be stimulated by Charlie, who exhausted him-self over the years in his never-ending donation of self.

To men of all stations, he was pal and tireless drinking companion. To women, he was a goal often achieved. He was sought after and not found wanting. He answered his own call, my Charlie did. Those who professed the greatest love for him turned his gifts into mere ornament.

Happiest at work, he wrote, when his admirers allowed him respite, plays that have lived. His work for the screen dignified the medium with a grace and sensibility too rarely found.

"Other men have to *do*, Helen. Charlie only has to *be*," Scott Fitzgerald said.

It is both true and false. True for everyone else, and false for Charlie. He wanted more. As a magician, with all his sleight of hand, he knew that something was slipping through his fingers. He was the writer who didn't have to write to be adored. This was his silent, gaily-borne torture.

Alec Woollcott knew this. When he heard of our plans to marry, he invited me one day to the Claremont Inn on River-side Drive to have some waffles, which, I was sure, were to be the Last Supper. As a drama critic, Alec had already ac-cepted me as an actress and so I had been spared his acid pen, which could so disfigure. So much for the credit side. Talent was far more important to Alec and his group than heart or character. Everything was Style.

I sat across the snowy cloth in something of a panic. I felt that anyone who had announced that the world would be a better place if it were peopled exclusively by MacArthurs would be hesitant to accept an addition who was not born one. But I was greatly surprised; Alec was in one of his sen-timental moods. His love of Charlie was genuine but, as I poured the maple syrup over my waffles and watched the pats of butter melt into golden puddles, Alec was doing the same over me. He couldn't have been kinder. I thought he was going to mock my romantic pretensions and my presumption for loving Prince Charming. Instead, he was trying to help me.

"Of all people, Helen, *you* know what it's like to live with that unhappiest of vaudeville teams—Haig and Haig."

I looked over his head at the Palisades across the river and I just listened.

"He's brilliant and quite mad. You, if I may observe, are quite balanced."

He seemed to be making sanity a vice.

"I know you love each other. Charlie's possessed with you, but he's also simply possessed. Can you live on the razor's edge, Helen? Do you really think that you can hang some chintz curtains on the lip of Vesuvius and call it home?"

"I know I can't give Charlie excitement," I now said slowly, "but he has enough for everybody. What I can give him—or die trying—is contentment and some degree of peace."

Alec sighed. We finished our breakfast in silence.

*   *   *

I had spent my first 28 years in the shadow of one dazzling, wayward creature called Brownie. Now I was about to spend the next 30 with another.

There is no point analyzing it, even if I could. Charlie and I couldn't have separated if we'd wanted to. And I won't deny there were times I prayed for release from him, going unwelcome to Church and praying that we both be saved from our love. But I might as well have prayed to wake up tall or an Eskimo or Mata Hari.

Charlie and I read a French play in rough translation years ago named *Auprès de ma blonde* by Marcel Achard.

Yvonne Printemps and Pierre Fresnay were playing it in Paris. It was about two quite ordinary people to whom a most extraordinary thing happened. They had found their own true loves in each other. According to the playwright this is a phenomenon that belongs only in grand opera and epic poetry since such an all-consuming passion makes demands beyond most mortals. These two people became a menace to their children, all those close to them, and even to themselves. The husband even took a mistress to release himself from the bondage; but there was no release, and the mistress was destroyed—not the marriage.

Their love was terrible and undignifying and to be ended only by death. Whether in heaven or hell, their marriage had been ordained; they came to accept their bondage.

We were mad about the drama and—at the time—had no idea that it curiously suggested our own. The most dire prophesies were fulfilled. The blackest predictions of my mother, my Church, and my friends cast a shadow over our sunny life. Yes, there was a dark side to the moon of my delight. But we could no more part from each other than change our natures.

More than once, when Charlie's demons dragged him from me, making me both a stranger and a witness to his self-destruction, I would think, *I'm through. I can't be expected to watch him destroy himself.* How often I thought that. How often I said it. But the mere repetition gives the lie to its sincerity.

I was much more honest when I announced, "If ever I threaten to leave you, Charlie, take no notice. It'll just be blather. You'll have to shoot me to get rid of me."

It was true. Still, there were times when I couldn't do the right thing, when sympathy was patronizing and lack of it devastating. On alternate Tuesdays, I accidentally achieved the proper balance. Other times when I raved about his talent in general or something sticking out of his typewriter in particular, I was in danger of going one word too far. Once he told me a bitter little story.

John Galsworthy's wife had complimented the playwright during a moment of self-doubt, and he had replied, "How wonderful to hear that from anybody else but a wife."

It is the writer's syndrome. I heard that Sir James Barrie eventually started talking his stories instead of writing them. I would have thought Barrie more stable than my entrancing scamp, who often escaped from labor and spread merriment instead; but it is alarming how all writers, no matter how prolific at the beginning, seem to peter out. Shaw was the exception; in his case, the drive outlived his genius.

Charlie would be off to his beautiful people.

"I'm studying them, Helen," he would say, on his way to El Morocco or Averell Harriman's. We knew we were both helpless.

During one of Charlie's fallow periods, my flourishing career underscored his wretchedness. After *Candle in the Wind,* I purposely quit for 18 months, concentrating on the children and Charlie. I was egocentric enough to think it was all my fault. My success made me guilty. But then the sight of me around the house only fed Charlie's guilt and robbed the children of the excitement they always found in my work. Both of them were to fall in love with the theatre. Both were to make it their careers.

Instead of concentrating on his own career, Charlie spent those 18 months finding me another vehicle. My last had been a failure.

Maxwell Anderson's anti-isolationist play *Candle in the Wind* was good propaganda and bad drama!

"You can't win a war with a bad play," was Charlie's only comment.

Before he joined the Army to do it in his own way, he set

out to find a good script which would satisfy my urge to be Joan of Arc.

"If you want to remind this country that we're in a helluva fix and better pull ourselves out of it, the way to do it from a stage is to go back to another time, when we were in a helluva fix and we *did* get out of it."

Charlie now spent night and day ploughing through biographies of great American women. Lo and behold! he came downstairs one morning bleary-eyed.

"I've got it. Harriet Beecher Stowe, housewife and mother, wrote a book that started the war that rid this country of slavery—who could ask for anything more?"

Once more one of those felicitous accidents that have propelled my career along occurred.

Our search for a script was not two months old when we heard that the University of Syracuse drama department was doing a couple of performances of a play called *Harriet*. We were on hand at the opening and, after the show, stunned the authors Ryerson and Clemens and ourselves by buying the play—on the spot. It was to be one of my greatest successes.

After a two-year run in New York, I toured in *Harriet*. For the first time, both children were at boarding schools—Mary at Rosemary Hall, Jim at Hill and Hallow. Colonel Mac-Arthur was in Washington. Mother was at the Croydon Hotel in Manhattan, and Daddy was in Maryland. The whole family was scattered across the country, and they were all happy that Mom was once again on the boards. I couldn't have retired if I'd wanted to. I learned that people become very upset if you act out of character.

Yes, my ego had made me believe that I was responsible for Charlie's sometime unhappiness with himself. Writers write from conviction or hunger. Charlie had told me that he was not temperamentally suited to be a writer.

"I have nothing to add to the endless minutes of this eternal meeting."

But there were many things within Charlie aching to be said and his failure to say them, his failure to write me a part that "would make Victoria look like a scullery maid," sent him escaping—to that merry-go-round which was his favorite method of travel and for which he had a season pass. It was quite a whirl until the carousel broke down.

Charlie reserved his genius for living, and it was both my gain and his era's. It is ironic that he gave me my identity and then clung to it, becoming so fused with me that my career became more important than his own. I suppose unconsciously he felt that when I was wrapped up in my work, I was less able to watch what he knew was the slow decline of his.

When he did write, he was magnificent. The World War I story, *Bug's Eye View of the World,* is considered a classic. Then with Ben Hecht the rough-and-ready memoir of their newspaper days, *Front Page,* which Tennessee Williams told me uncorseted the American theatre with its earthy, two-fisted vitality; the zany, urbane *Twentieth Century,* based on Charlie's experiences with the great Belasco. Then unlike so many others, Charlie and Ben Hecht broke away from Hollywood for a while, writing and producing their own pictures in the East—little masterpieces, like *The Scoundrel,* starring Noel Coward, and *Crime Without Passion,* with Claude Rains. He and Ben produced some real gems.

Even when they returned to Hollywood—there among the moguls and the minions—all that irritation produced some pearls. One of their finest was *Wuthering Heights.*

❋   ❋   ❋

Charlie was seduced by Hollywood. So were Scott Fitzgerald and Aldous Huxley and William Faulkner. I'll never forget Faulkner in his cubbyhole at MGM, or Dorothy Parker in hers after she painted the word MEN on the door.

These cubbyholes were considered solitary confinement to these free souls, and Dottie's sign was a plea for guests. Hers was the only office that wasn't a lonely place.

Many writers were misused out there in Hollywood, but Charlie was really bruised. Routine and pressures were not for him. He and Ben never met a deadline in Hollywood. An odd development in two legendary newspapermen.

I remember once some MGM producer calling on the hour for a script that Charlie was supposed to have finished weeks before. The tension had blocked him completely.

Instead of being in his cubbyhole, he was playing tennis at the Beverly Hills courts. The nervous producer tracked him down and got him on the phone.

"I want that script *today*, MacArthur," he screamed. "And no alibis! It's now or never! It's today or else!" And he hung up.

Charlie drove to the studio straight from the courts, went to his cubbyhole, gathered up at random all the papers he happened to find—including the day's mail—and carried the impressive bundle to the mogul's office. As he sailed in, he held the mess of papers high in the air.

"I could give you these right now," he said grandly. "Deadlines are the easiest things to meet. But this script isn't *worthy* of you. A man of *your* standards!"

With which, he dramatically tore up his "creation" under the nose of the gaping producer. No one has ever been so conscientious in destroying a work of art. He didn't stop until each sheet was in unreadable shreds. He tossed the confetti into the air and happily returned to finish his tennis game.

It's a wonder anything ever got done in Hollywood. All the creative people were to be found at the Beverly Hills Courts. Charlie actually found his Heathcliff there.

"Helen, on the other side of the net today, there was the perfect Heathcliff. A real brooding gypsy of a boy. Brontë would swoon if she could see him."

"What's his name?"

"Larry Olivier or something."

"But that's the boy who played *you* in Sam Behrman's *No Time for Comedy*."

S. N. Behrman had called a year before and asked if we would mind if he based his leading character on Charlie—a playwright married to a star, who was to be played by Katherine Cornell. On the basis of his appearance in the play, the boy was called to Hollywood.

Charlie was so impressed with this beautiful young man that he convinced Sam Goldwyn to hire him. He could not, however, swing it for the young man's sweetheart. The young man thought she could make a divine Cathy, but Goldwyn balked.

"You made me take one unknown. Now you want me to use *two*. And it's a doubtful picture anyway."

Merle Oberon was absolutely lovely in that masterpiece of film-making, but Vivien Leigh did not remain unknown for long.

Ben and Charlie returned East to complete that film and created another legend in the process. Alec Woollcott had insisted that the boys come to his country place to work on the screen-play. *Wuthering Heights* was one of his "favorite confections"—and he was damned if he was going to stand by and let these Katzenjammer Kids mutilate it.

Charlie and Ben accepted his invitation only after they took time out to write a dummy scene meant only for Alec's eye. They had Heathcliff come to America and fight Indians and cattle rustlers in Red Rock Gulch, with a gun on each hip and a dance-hall hostess in tow.

Knowing that Alec was a congenital snooper, they left the scene lying where he would find it.

"Oafs! Clods! Vandals! You have raped Emily Bronte!" Alec shrieked.

"She's been waiting breathlessly for years," Charlie answered simply.

It is both testament to Hecht and MacArthur's greatness and to Hollywood's reputation that Alexander Woollcott, critic *extraordinaire*, could believe such a jest.

❂ ❂ ❂

Charlie's escapes from reality became more frequent as the years went on. But good or bad, every moment was still dipped in gold. It just came naturally to my alchemist.

Charlie was created for the *beau geste*. He could always rise to the great occasion. It was between the valiant acts that Charlie got lost. He needed to be heroic.

War offered him his release. There, he could traffic in the clear-cut excesses of good and evil. It was there he knew which side to be on. All senses were heightened and he could, like Hemingway at the bullfight, feel the exquisite agony of near-death and then be guiltily grateful for survival.

Heavy fisted and overly brave, darkly handsome, my black Scot—whom Walt Kuhn wanted to paint as a faun—was more of a James Montgomery Flagg recruiting poster, an illustration of the romantic warrior.

Yes, the broad stroke was his specialty, the minutia of daily life his undoing. It sent him reeling out into the night. Reality was too much for my mother; it was not enough for my Charlie.

Living with him made me shock-proof. He turned me, over the years, into a woman who could take anything.

Like the couple in the Achard play, we were meant for each other and all else fell into place. Our story had to play itself out to the end, no matter what. We were doomed to stay together—beautifully doomed.

When we married and returned to the scene of Charlie's childhood, buying a house in Nyack and raising a family, I was to know the golden years.

12

ARRIAGE is like a war. There are moments of chivalry and gallantry that attend the victorious advances and strategic retreats, the birth or death of children, the momentary conquest of loneliness, the sacrifice that ennobles him who makes it. But mostly there are the long dull sieges, the waiting, the terror and boredom. Women understand this better than men; they are better able to survive attrition.

Eric Linklater said that women know how to inhabit the world and men never seem to feel at home on it. I saw it with my own children.

Jamie as a little boy flexed his tiny muscles and started to fight the world immediately. Mary looked about her and serenely settled in. Maybe all women have been here before. We, the battle-scarred, humbly say to the new recruits—the unyielding young women who no longer have the patience for such a life—"Don't forfeit your role because the sacrifices

171

seem large." I believe the totally free women are the wretched ones. The captive submissive hearts are usually more fulfilled.

With Charlie, I was half travel agent and half plumber. Though I depended on Charlie for his love and his decisions, though he created our garden, our house, our life—even me —I was kept hopping with details. I was never a diva at home. Charlie was.

Being an actress, I have always been a quick-change artist. I can dress and be out of the house in jig time. My husband never had to wait for me to finish dressing in his whole life. It was I who waited nightly.

Charlie was like the late Jimmy Walker, the popular and ever-tardy Mayor of New York. He was just never on time. Woollcott would not take that kind of inconsideration, even from his pet, and one day, when Charlie arrived to pick him up for lunch about an hour late, Alec's man made the great one's rage only too clear.

"Mr. Woollcott will not allow me to tell you where he's lunching. And he said for you not to call him. He'll call you —next year. I'm sorry, Mr. MacArthur."

"So am I," Charlie answered, sadly as a parent about to deliver a spanking.

He went off to the nearest A & P where he bought fifty packages of assorted flavors of Jello and lugged them back to Alec's place, where he managed to gain re-entrance. He then poured every package into the bathtub and turned on the hot water. When the Jello had dissolved, he filled the tub.

At another time, Alec invited us to Voisin for dinner with the Grand Duchess Marie of Russia and Harpo Marx of Hollywood and again we were late. Arriving at the restaurant, we were directed by the maitre d', not to Woollcott's table, where the master was characteristically riveting everyone's attention with an anecdote, but to a corner table for two. This was our exile.

Charlie helped me to my seat. "Waiter," he announced, "we would like your best Beluga caviar, Coquille St. Jacques, Saumon Fumée, Chateaubriand. . . ."

"Charlie," I protested, "are you mad? I can't eat all of that."

"Just put your fork in everything and mess it around. Old King Cole is going to pay for this in spades."

But Charlie didn't always have the last word. When I was about to give birth to Mary and he was finishing up a job in Hollywood, he decided to return to New York, not by train, but for some mysterious reason through the Panama Canal. It was his whim. He took a passenger ship of the United Fruit Line, deciding to rest up for a couple of weeks.

When the ship landed in Havana, Charlie went ashore and toured the bars. When he returned to the dock, heaven knows how much later, the ship was gone. He was outraged that they dared depart without him. Stranded with white flannels, a tennis sweater, and a hangover, he phoned Anita Loos in Palm Beach to cable him some money.

He called me from Miami. Anita had staked him to the train fare back to New York.

"Meet me at Penn Station with some proper clothes, will you, Helen—with an overcoat and galoshes?"

Of course, I did. I'll never forget our standing there on that freezing winter's day, travelers giving us a wide berth as they stared at Charlie—tanned and handsome all in white —a juvenile caught in a musical comedy crisis. And me, seven months pregnant, for all the world the second-act complication.

❋   ❋   ❋

Charlie's legend and mine were always at cross-purposes.

I was being called the First Lady of the American Theatre—
sharing the dubious title with Kit Cornell and Lynn; and
Charlie the irreverent, who had spent his whole life aiming
snowballs at silk hats, now had the perfect target right there
at home.

When my career first took me to Hollywood, I made a
series of wildly successful films. My first, *Madelon Claudet*,
which Charlie wrote for me, won me an Oscar. Movies give
you a wider fame and more possessive audience and I started
to complain that my face was too easily recognized.

"The price is too great, Charlie," I bemoaned. "I can't
move. I can't shop. I can't wander or do a single thing without everybody gaping at me."

When I returned to New York, I kept going on about it.
Fame and adulation were just too much for me.

"Stop giving yourself such airs," Charlie scolded.

"But I'm not, Charlie," I protested. "You'll see today. It's
just awful. I'll never have any privacy again."

We were at our apartment at 25 East End Avenue and we
walked across to Park and Tilford's on Fifth Avenue, where
Tiffany's now stands. Not a soul bothered me. No one even
knew I was alive.

"Keep a cool head, Helen. We'll fix them." Charlie said.

He dropped behind me and started hobbling on one foot,
loudly proclaiming:

> Old Mother Witch
> Lived in a ditch
> Picked up a penny
> And thought she was rich.

And he was pointing a crooked finger at me as he hobbled
along. They were all looking now, for sure.

That's how seriously I was allowed to take myself around
my Charlie.

Both of us were to be captives of our growing legends. Charlie's was more colorful, but it was to destroy him. Mine was duller but kinder; it allowed me to prevail.

George Kaufman had been right about the strange casting. One night, attending theatre with Ben and Rose Hecht and a dear Hollywood friend named Charlie Lederer and his date, we walked down the aisle at a musical hit. My arrival was noticed most gratifyingly by the rest of the audience. I smiled graciously, in response to the patter of applause, but on that rainy, rainy night I felt in my bones that there was even rougher weather ahead.

My heart began to sink when the two Charlies removed their wet shoes. We were sitting near the tympani and Charlie Lederer spread his damp socks over the bass drum to dry. He now turned to his shocked and elegantly dressed neighbor.

"Wet socks could cause a rheumatic pain that might kill my high kicks."

"Humph!" was the lady's disinterested response.

"Doctor Kronkeit is a far better guide to the joy that comes from health than Emily Post," my Charlie agreed loyally.

"It's better with your shoes off," continued the other Charlie.

Between the two of them, I sank lower and lower in my seat, while Rose and Ben made believe they were in another theatre. Lederer continued filling the hapless lady's ear with his absurd confidences, until she handed the problem over to her strapping escort. He began threatening Lederer and then, on his wife's insistence, left to get the usher.

"You might as well take a good pinch, Lederer," my Elizabethan husband now suggested. "We're going to be thrown out anyway."

The First Lady of the American Theatre was asked to

leave it that evening. We made our exit and I was ready to keep going.

"I can't go on this way, Charlie, Don't you realize how mortifying——"

"Don't make a case for yourself, Helen," Charlie smiled. "Things are bad all over!"

"Charlie. . . ."

" 'The whol' worl', Juno, is in a terr—ible state of chassis.' " Thus spoke my Paycock! And that was that.

The next morning, Charlie Lederer sent me a coffin-sized box of gorgeous chrysanthemums from Max Schling. No one in that crowd ever just did something. It was always in Technicolor and Panavision. Harpo Marx, on my marriage, had sent me a Steinway piano crate filled with fresh gardenias.

Now I had a non-contrite husband and a coffin of chrysanthemums. I felt it was for my dead career.

Charlie never voiced regret for one moment of mischief.

"Aren't you sorry, Charlie? Not *that* much?"

"But why, Helen? Poor Lederer could have got the ague."

He still didn't know about my rest-in-peace offering. That was my trump card.

"Well, even your maniacal, hypochondriacal Lederer has had the grace to be sorry, and a very sweet and expensive apology it is." I dragged him out of bed and marched him to the monstrous gift.

Charlie remained unimpressed. All I wanted was a crumb of remorse but, at least, I got grim satisfaction. At the end of the month, we received a sky-high bill from Max Schling. Lederer had charged the flowers to us.

* * *

Charlie was the perfect iconoclast. Starting at the top, he worked his way down to us mortals, missing no one who had more airs than he thought necessary for survival. If he had ever met the buoyant Professor Piccard, I am certain that he would have pricked his balloon as he did so many others.

He was appalled, with justification, by Elsie Janis's "Ma"— the ultimate stage mother—without whom Elsie couldn't have breathed. This woman did everything but take her daughter's bows. She had the misfortune of becoming overbearing with Charlie at a party. She came out second best.

When she, on leaving, gave him a chance to apologize, Charlie simply said, "You don't understand, Madame. I was sent by God to be rude to you."

On another occasion, stopping a supercilious and malicious hostess from tearing a friend to shreds, he reminded her that she, too, had been caught in what he called "fragrant delight." When Bob Benchley asked him how he could have been so devastating, his answer was characteristic.

"She was too enthroned."

That answer had endeared him so to Bob when they first met that they became inseparable. Singly, each was an urbane and witty man; together, they became a menace to society. Their only exercise was the walk from their bachelor flat to the nearest bar. On one of their three-minute hikes from their apartment to "21," they caught sight of the aristocratic Justice Charles Evans Hughes. I blush to relate that these two adults actually pointed at his great beard and yelled "Beaver! King Beaver! It's the granddaddy of them all!" The Chief Justice of the Supreme Court—who swore in Presidents! I shudder still.

As long as I can remember, I wanted to grow up. My Charlie died a little boy. Throughout his life, he clung, along with Ben Hecht and other cronies, to a dream of eternal boyhood where villains and heroes are easily distinguishable, where fun is always to be had and responsibilities are to be shrugged away. This was the nature of him and I have no complaints. I guess I loved being a mother. Mother's needs taught me how.

Charlie was a good father. Mary and Jamie adored him—and why wouldn't they have? He shared with all other children the love of the outrageous.

Miss Astrid, Mary's Norwegian governess, had an easy time with her charge. There were other forces at work in the house that disturbed her. Straitlaced and prudish, a professional gentlewoman, she was a strain on Charlie. He would endure her so long and then wham!

But one night at dinner I was as shocked as little six-year-old Mary was delighted.

Her father suddenly said, "I would like to teach you to shoot mashed potatoes, Mary."

The rest of the table froze.

"This trick comes in very handy," he continued. "You see, when you're at table, Mary, and find that someone is talking too much or is a little too stuffy, argument is stupid—and we all know that sulking is most unattractive in young ladies. One must approach the situation with subtlety. So the only thing to do is put a generous helping of mashed potatoes on a spoon, turn the spoon around—thusly—then take your little thumb—and place it at the back of the spoon—and with a flick of your wrist——"

I really do not think that Charlie meant to hit Miss Astrid smack in the face with those mashed potatoes, but as she sat dignified and dripping he became convulsed with laughter. He may not have planned it, but he was awfully pleased when it happened.

How could Mary not have adored this playmate? When Jim came along, Charlie had a real partner in crime. My two men always had their heads together and I, as well as the rest of the world, was the butt of their mischief.

At one point, understandably between servants, I decided to make my first Thanksgiving dinner. It was going to be my triumph, and I took the chore seriously. I warned Charlie and Jim that if the turkey didn't turn out just right, if it was raw or tasteless or whatever could happen to a turkey in the hands of an amateur, I would not countenance ridicule. This feast was going to be an all-day job and I wanted some compassion. If it didn't work out well, we would simply go to St. George's Inn up the road, but we would not make sport of Mother.

"I want no jokes, no gags. Just remember that."

"Good luck," was all Charlie would say.

It was beginner's luck: the turkey was perfect, its golden-crusted, snowy meat only equalled by the chestnut dressing. I was as proud as Punch and shouted, "Dinner's ready," knowing that those hungry boys would adore the meal and shower me with praise. I brought the platter in and there they were, completely dressed for the trek to the Inn—overcoats, boots, mittens, and wide grins.

* * *

Charlie was irrepressible, his high spirits and panache leading him to excesses that would simulate the glory of battle. There was violence in my Charlie—blessedly withheld from family. He reserved all hostility for war and certain men—some of them his friends.

He was the gentlest of lovers and the kindest of fathers, except for that time when Jamie, then five, climbed out on the window ledge of Charlie's study and started crawling toward the rainpipe. He got a walloping for that. But Charlie at home only showed the peak of the iceberg.

His lips would become thin, his cheek muscles would twitch. The voice was soft in volume and hard in timbre. He could seethe with rage and when he did his strong arms and large hands corded with tension. There was indeed an anger within him and one could feel it, like the rumble of an earth-quake beneath the surface. Some were to know his violence well.

I had heard of past fights—how Charlie had knocked out his managing editor in the old Chicago, Walter Howey days; how he knocked three cabbies for a loop simultaneously for some forgotten reason; and how, in a friendly match, he had sent Ernest Hemingway to his knees, though Ernest later denied it so vociferously that the two writers almost started it all over again. I have survived them both and am here to report that Philip Barry and Scott Fitzgerald assured me—as if it really mattered—that Charlie won in a breeze.

It is impossible to count the gatherings we were forced to leave because Charlie had decided to defend a point of view by punching someone in the jaw. Charlie was easily of-fended. My pleas, exasperation, my impatience availed me nothing.

Charlie couldn't look at David Selznick without hitting him. It was, as Cole Porter said, just one of those things. One too many and he was off. Selznick's mere presence was suffi-cient. Charlie would look at him and the rest was reflex.

One night at Harpo Marx's, I was talking to Myron Selz-nick, who suddenly said, "Is it all right for my brother and your husband to be chatting?"

"Myron," I said, "just look at them. They're getting along like a house on fire."

Not one minute passed before the house fell in. Pow! Bang! There wasn't a raised voice and most of the guests just continued their conversations, but my heart stopped. David and Charlie were rolling on the thick carpeted floor like tigers. No one will ever know why. It might have been the iodine in the air. We were again among the first to leave a social gathering.

I must add that when Charlie died and, at the simplest of ceremonies, I had his dear friend and collaborator, Ben Hecht, say a few words, David Selznick was discovered upstairs in the overflow crowd at the funeral parlor. He was weeping like a child. Men are strange and wonderful beings.

When my husband once, in Hollywood, was brought home early from another shindig that I could not attend because of a film schedule, I again berated him. I was at the end of my rope.

"What now, Charlie? Who now?"

"Victor Mature," Charlie answered, as if that were sufficient explanation.

"What does that mean, Charlie? When is this going to end?"

"You don't understand," he answered. "The guy just begged for it."

"You mean he asked you to hit him?"

"He stood there, being Victor Mature."

"And now, announcing the main event," I said bitterly. "Mature vs. Immature!"

"Helen, no man has a right to look that way. I had to hit him. There isn't a court in the land that would convict me."

"Oh, yes, there is," said I.

A few years later, we went to see Gertrude Lawrence in *Lady in the Dark* on Broadway with Maurice Evans and Mady Christian. When Victor Mature, in Eliza's fantasy, walked on stage in his pink tights, he was such a gorgeous muscular soufflé of a man that I suddenly understood everything. Right is right and I stood up immediately, leaned across Maurice and Mady, and extended my hand.

"Put it there, Charlie. My apologies."

He rose and we shook hands ceremoniously before we resumed our seats.

When *The Robe* was being filmed, Victor Mature appeared with Richard Burton in the Hollywood epic. He played a Christian slave who, because of his beliefs, is thrown into the arena with a lion. His faith quells the beast. The actor was certain that a double was going to be used for this scene, but such was not the plan. When the lion was led onto the set, the director started discussing the mechanics of the scene with Victor, who was incredulous.

"You must think I'm out of my mind," he protested.

"You don't understand, Victor," the director purred, "He's a poor dilapidated old pussycat. Leo's grandpa."

Victor took a good look at the old beast and still saw the heaving, golden mass of power, the shaggy matted head, restless, suspicious, and hungry.

"He looks extremely fit to me," the actor observed.

"But of course, Victor. The audience has to believe he's ferocious. But we know that he's had enough sedation to kill a dozen starlets, *and—*" he continued in a conspiratorial whisper, delivering the clincher, "he doesn't have one tooth in his mouth."

"Well, who the hell wants to be gummed to death?" Victor ended the conversation.

I changed my mind about Victor Mature after that, and Charlie would have too. That line deserved a pat on the back and not a punch on the jaw.

As a matter of fact, Jim recently told me, after all these years, that Charlie confessed to him in one of their gabfests that he didn't knock Mature down. He tried, but couldn't. That creature, who was known in Hollywood as "a beautiful hunk of man," kept standing like a pretty brick wall. The years were taking their toll and father admitted to son, if not to me, that he was getting a bit long in the tooth and might consider hanging up his gloves. It was none too soon.

* * *

Charlie and Jim had a fine relationship. They had it from the moment they met, in that hospital where Charlie picked him up the day of adoption. The infant took one look at his new father and wouldn't take his eyes off him. Flattered and committed forever, Charlie forgot his admonition to me before I gave birth to Mary.

"Make it a girl, Helen. I don't want any little son of a so-and-so giving me any competition."

His adoration of our Mary was to be boundless, made up of gentleness and mischief. It was always playtime and Charlie's eyes shone with the joy of her. Mary was not only beautiful; she was a serene and old soul from the very beginning.

I wanted more children. I wanted a dozen, but it wasn't to be. I was obsessed with my failure, and Charlie and I went through the usual witchcraft to no avail.

My frustration was terrible, and the migraines that followed led my doctor to suggest our adopting a second child. That we did, to our everlasting pleasure.

Mary worshiped the new baby; that spunky, impish little boy was to be her happy slave and often my Nemesis. That miniature man dashing about the house, bright and sassy, breaking rules and other precious things, crashing his way into boyhood, brash and candid, utterly lacking in guile, was to enrich our lives more than we ever could his.

Jamie was always a man, from the very pink-and-white beginning, and this is what Charlie responded to. They never played baseball or camped or fished together. Charlie was too honest simply to play the concept of a father; he was too authentic. He hated exercise; he said he'd got a lifetime of it walking through three wars. Though he wouldn't discourage it in his son, he saw no need to share it.

What he did give Jim was far more important. He gave him the companionship of the mind and the trust of mutual confidence. They played chess together and they talked together. They competed for my attention, they squabbled, they made up, and they confided in each other like the friends they were.

When the principal of Jim's school asked me at one point what kind of relationship Jim's father had with him I could answer, "His father talks to him. And his father talks real good."

Charlie would come to bed filled with such confidences that this unshockable man was stunned .

"Helen, I wouldn't dream—*I* wouldn't dream—of repeating what that kid told me this evening. Of course, it's great that it's out of *his* system—but now it's in mine." He would laugh. "Kids are fantastic."

And such was their intimacy. Charlie and Jim were both demonstrative, eager to love and be loved. As a small boy, mischievous as he was, Jamie would suddenly and shyly slip a little gift in my hand. I remember silver salt and pepper shakers which he bought after a month of saving his 25¢ weekly allowance. He had seen them in the window of Womrath's Book and Gift Shop. Every day of that long month he would fearfully approach that window to see if they were still there. He was certain that everyone else in town coveted them.

That same little imp would follow me around like a puppy, and, when I would at last drop what I was doing, he would trip me up or knock me over. That was back-breaking.

There was a time I decided that Jamie was far too secure,

that some book-burning was in order. I had quite a time with that boy, after being spoiled by the gentle Mary. She, in turn, now defended her brother's every fall from grace with a dedication usually reserved for a holy crusade.

It is true that Jamie's loving nature was warming. He would suddenly stop whatever he was doing to hug or kiss me. His curly golden head was that of an angel; it was the cloven hoof that would trip you up.

"Mom, Mom! Take a taste of my delicious eggnog. Mom, *please* have some of my eggnog."

He was about five years old and my little shadow.

"No, Darling," I would keep saying with diminishing sweetness, "not now. Mom's just had her breakfast."

"*Please*, Mom. Have just a *teeny* sip."

"*Please*, Jamie. No, not now."

His stick-to-it-iveness seemed anything but a virtue, but then I remembered one of the tomes I'd read after achieving motherhood. *What am I doing to this cherub's psyche? Am I out of my mind?* I thought. *If it means that much to the child and it's such a giving sign . . .*

"How kind you are, Darling. How thoughtful, Jamie. Of course I'll have a little of your eggnog."

I took the colorful mug and lifted it to my lips; whereupon my son reached up and gave the mug a sudden smack from underneath sending the eggnog all over me. The chase that followed was of comic-strip intensity. I thank God that he was always able to outrun me—otherwise he might never have grown up.

Jamie enraged and enchanted and eventually exhausted the rest of us. Only his beloved Mary was spared by the little brat. When Charlie and I had Bunty Cobb MacNaughton's little boy Charles stay with us during the London Blitz, he and Jamie became minikin and manikin, monkey see, monkey do. They were inseparable. They were ganging up on the dogs, the servants, and me. Too infrequently would they go at each other, a most welcome sight.

One day, the two kids were particularly obnoxious to one of the dogs, and I, in despair, remembered something my sister-in-law Helen Bishop had told me. When she was small and the children in the house were being naughty, her mother used to gather them to her knee and say, "I have been a terrible mother. If I were a good mother, you would all be good children and wouldn't be doing all these terrible things. I've been so bad as a mother that I want you to punish me."

She would then direct her plea to the ringleader.

"Hit me, Darling. No, I mean it. I deserve to be hit."

Her loving children would start whimpering, "No, no, Mother, please, we'll be good. We're *sorry!*" When she forced one of them to give her a token slap, a great wail would go up and all the imps would cling to their mother, begging for forgiveness. After they had comforted her and she them, they would go off, red-eyed and chastened.

I was absolutely touched by this charming cure; it was so creative. Jamie was racing around like an Indian, smacking Turvey's bottom with a stick. It was in the midst of their cookie feud.

"Jamie!" I beckoned. "Come here, Darling."

He and his little partner in crime cautiously approached me. I was at the pool, sitting in a low beach chair in my bathing suit.

"Don't be afraid, Jamie. I want to talk to you."

The boys stood at my side as I rested my book on my lap.

I repeated the Georgianna MacArthur dialogue—ending sanctimoniously with "If you must hit someone, hit me, your wicked mother, not poor Turvey!"

Jamie pulled his ear to make sure he had heard correctly. His eyes were round with disbelief. What he usually heard was the maternal, "If you do not leave that poor animal alone, I will kick you to kingdom come."

This was all strange to Jamie—a brand-new mom. Our English house guest had all the innocence of the Artful Dodger.

"Hit her, Jamie," he encouraged my son. "Go on and hit her."

I could have slapped him.

"Yes, I deserve it, Jamie. I've been a bad mother."

It was beautiful: Jamie was rendered utterly helpless. He just stared at me.

"She told you to hit her," young MacNaughton pressed on. "Go ahead and hit her."

Jamie was roused from his reverie. He turned to his friend and then to me. I felt like Mae Marsh in *Over the Hill*—all cameo, lace dickey, and work-worn-motherhood. My son picked up the stick with which he had been harassing Turvey, took a low swing, and cracked me across the shins with all his might. Those two monsters were only saved by the time it took me to rouse myself from my ungainly position. I was considering murder.

I could never catch him. It was Charles who got the chance to use the hairbrush.

The only time I ever lay in wait for Jim—when he was about 13 and Charlie was out of town—my temper, as usual, paralyzed me. He was out with his darling friend Philip Glynne—and I'd asked him to get home early, "when Philip does, Dear." But Jamie had started the battle of the sexes at the age of six months and wasn't taking any orders. I sat up in fear and fury, after calling the Glynnes to hear that Philip had come home long before. I turned out all the lights and sat myself in the front hall, like Maggie waiting for Jiggs. I had all the determination, though I had left the rolling pin in the kitchen.

When the door opened and Jim walked in, I switched on the lights and jumped up and charged. As he ducked and fled my flailing arms I heard myself screaming—of all things —"You wretched fellow!" I make no sense when I lose my temper.

* * *

My powers of speech become remarkably affected and I just don't say what I mean. Once in Hollywood I had such an outburst.

I was making Sinclair Lewis's *Arrowsmith* with Ronald Colman. The screenplay was written by Pulitzer Prize winner Sidney Howard, who had written *Salvation* with Charlie. I respected his talent and was appalled when our director, John Ford, started to hack away at some scenes.

"Look, Jack," I said, "you're rewriting Sidney Howard. When Goldwyn sees it we're only going to have to do the whole business over again."

"And who is directing this picture?" he asked me.

He had promised Sam Goldwyn that he would stay on the wagon until he was through with this film and his patience was wearing thin. He was actually very fond of me, but his tone now became ferocious.

"Get on that set and stick to your acting—such as it is!"

Instead of following his direction I barely managed to return to my canvas camp chair. I flopped into it just before my legs gave way.

I was blinded, incapacitated, consumed with rage. I couldn't move. Jack Ford did. He walked slowly over to me chewing the corner of his handkerchief, which was *his* sign of stress.

"What's the matter, Honey? Did I upset you?"

Now was my chance to put him in his place. I drew myself up.

"I am not accustomed to being speaken to in that manner," I said loud and clear.

There was an appreciative pause before the titters started and rapidly grew into pandemonium. Grips fell off parapets, makeup men and script girls were reduced to hysteria. Yes-men stopped saying yes.

I prayed for oblivion. This prayer unanswered, I settled for laughter. Both Jack and I now joined the general merriment. I am not effective when agitated.

*   *   *

What a comfort it has been having Jim. Through it all, starting with his sister's death and his father's illness, he has always been there when I've needed him.

I resented his becoming burdened at such an age. I dreaded becoming dependent, dreaded being the bereft widow with the captive son. My terror, at one point, of using Jim caused me, in a sense, to reject him. Jim's manly need to protect was something I couldn't exploit. His great attachment to me could not be encouraged. Rather, I felt, it was more important that that strength be used to build his own family and his own life.

We must all, eventually, stand alone. In Charlie's last years, Jim tended him through shingles, kidney ailments, ulcers, and self-denigration. Jim's devotion was unbelievable, and now he was prepared to be my bastion.

Jim was made to give, but all my training made me an inept taker. I think relationships should be sculptural—have space around them. Charlie and I allowed each other to breathe.

It wasn't lack of love for my son that made me decide to return to work after Charlie died. It was my way of freeing him of the burden of my widowhood.

Talented Jamie, following his sister's footsteps and en-

couraged by her, had already appeared on television with
great success as *The Young Stranger*. The die was cast and
now Jim started his film career and blessedly founded his
own family. Charlie and I, with all our fears and all our
mistakes, had managed to bring up a man.

His little boy, my grandson Charles, saw *The White Sister*
on television and announced to his classmate, John Gable,
"I saw your father kissing my grandma the other night."
And so the world moves on and we cannot stop it. I have
lived in the happy belief that my life has been magnificent.
Notwithstanding all the crises, it is true that for some time
it was charmed.

Even Father's story ended happily, though Mother's did
not. She had concentrated on the ideal, refusing to accept
fact. Jean Dixon had remained with her for a couple of years
until she was over the shock of my marriage. On Jean's own
admission she needed Mother as much as she herself was
needed. Presented with one grandchild and then another
Mother really couldn't hurdle the generations though she
tried. She stayed with us whenever possible.

But Charlie had taken over my life and Mother couldn't
put together the jigsaw puzzle of her own. All the creature
comforts couldn't turn the trick, but she attempted—often
succeeding—to be gay and to encourage some young hopeful.

Her last favorite, Laura May Church, ironically was sent
to her by Father, who hoped Brownie would look after the
daughter of a friend.

Laura May moved in and happily remained with Mother
until her own marriage—to Gene Mako, the tennis cham-
pion. Even beyond Mother's lifetime, Lari Mako holds her
up as her idol.

Everyone's sacrifice made me a success, and my success
made many things possible. My father was able to spend
his last years in a snug house on Chesapeake Bay, with a

garden he could tend, a devoted housekeeper to cook him outrageously fattening meals, and a man to do the heavy work and collect the great bay oysters for his Lucullan feasts.

He had many cronies; they would argue international vagaries and umpires' decisions, literally sitting on cracker barrels outside the drygoods store in the village of Pierson, Maryland. I pray that he was somewhat repaid for his years of emotional want. He was to know the delight of his grandchildren when he stayed with us in Nyack or we visited him on the Bay, and he was able to listen to me on the radio every week as he gloated in front of his friends. Radio had made my name a household word in the smallest hamlet, and that pleased him more than any theatrical acclaim or fulfillment, which was really beyond him.

I think he was proudest of my "unactress-ish" private life. He was astonished and filled with pride that I had been able to come through the darkest regions of Broadway and Hollywood with my respectability intact. I was told that my father used to boast that "mah daughtuh nevah has appeahed in a piece that was impropuh." Well, it wasn't because I didn't want to. But those in power always saw me as a noble innocent. A long list of such parts created the image that doomed me forever to public purity. I was to go from gingham virgin to the Statue of Liberty in a Mother Hubbard—sacrosanct to the general public and saccharine anathema to the *cognoscenti*.

Although there have been times I have decried this blandest of roles, I have not really felt the urge to rebel. This was the part of me I inherited from Francis Van Arnum Brown. Like him, I accepted the part in which the Fates cast me and I have played it the best way I know how.

Carlyle said:

> Let each become all that
> He was created able of being

> Expand, if possible, to his full growth
> And show himself at length
> In his own shape and stature
> Be these what they may.

Father lived it. I have tried to.

*   *   *

When I look back over these years, a holiday mood possesses me. Charlie and I had everything for a while. Each other would have been enough, but then there were the children, the endless stream of intoxicating friends, energy, and a never-ceasing supply of money. We were so terribly extravagant. We really lived it up, Charlie and I.

There were times when I went to work in *Victoria* on our own boat, cruising down the Hudson from our great sprawling house in Nyack—which Charlie Lederer named Pretty Penny—to the 79th Street dock, lunching or cocktailing with our guests like royalty. We had more servants than residents. Mixing queens if not metaphors, I was Victoria on her barge.

We spent our money as quickly as we made it. After 15 years of this free-wheeling, Charlie's brilliant financier of a brother, Alfred MacArthur, made us scrape together what we had left the morning after, so he could invest it for us. It was 25 years ago that Alfred began insuring our future—a task that came naturally to him since he owned about 15 insurance companies.

Alfred invested the pittance we had in all sorts of romantic stocks that he knew would please me. Railroads and hotels because I love travel, and property because I'm Irish and love the land. When Charlie died, his family stepped in to see me through. They're quite a clan, those MacArthurs. One gave me my life, the others saved it.

The old deacon certainly whipped a mighty drive into three-quarters of his sons. But John, the financier, Telfer, the publisher, and Alfred would be the first to admit that it was Charlie who made us all richer.

＊　＊　＊

There was always a party. When our Mary was one year old, Charlie decided we should have a huge celebration. We were staying at our apartment in town on East End Avenue, which we kept for years.

"Let's have a real shindig," Charlie said. "I mean a real humdinger. Let's have everybody!"

Charlie's enthusiasm was as contagious as the measles.

"All right. Where do we begin?"

"With the A's, of course," he answered.

He threw me a pad and pencil. "And we stay with it to the bitter end."

"Is Alec an A or a W?" I asked. "Ephraim is going to be a Z, because I can't think of another one except Zimbalist."

"Alec is a lovable, pompous S. But we'd better get some order into this thing and just use last names.''

We put our feet up on the coffee table and gathered up all the exciting people we knew and loved to share our happiness. Then Charlie said, "Asking them to Mary's birthday is going to sound like ice cream and cake and nobody will come, so let's be original. But first let's see how our peers are doing it."

We went through our unanswered invitations to parties and all of them seemed to be in honor of Prince Whatchamacallit or Countess Something-or-Other, an English novelist or Swedish scientist. Everybody that season seemed to be honoring some lion.

"I know," my husband said, grabbing the pencil. He scrawled a simple invitation. "Now listen. 'Helen and Charles MacArthur request the honour'—with a 'u,' of course—'of your august presence on the fifteenth of February to meet

Scarface Al Capone. R.S.V.P.' I think that's great. How does it sound to you?"

"I'm impressed," I answered.

We had the invitations printed and sent out, and as Bea Lillie would—and did—say, "It was a mahvelous party."

Only Lucrezia Bori took the joke seriously and asked, as she was removing her wrap, where Capone was. Her snapping, black eyes kept darting around the apartment in search of the gangster. She loved Charlie, but when he told her it was all a jest, she bridled. She refused to believe Capone wasn't there. When at last she was convinced, she became a blazing doña.

"I have come to meet this 15th-century *bandido* that you have promised and look who is here—the civilized and the famous. Charlie, I insist. You couldn't cheat me. Where is he?"

Lucrezia would not let up. Charlie's little joke had backfired. La Bori had Capone on the brain, and her rage kept growing as she nourished it. Charlie had met his match—she was all aflame.

Charlie could never let a lady down. He went to the telephone and called an old Chicago friend of his newspaper days there—the mobster's lawyer.

"Look, I'm in a spot. I have a crazy diva here who'll put the evil eye on me if she can't meet Capone. She's got to talk to him. What do you mean, he doesn't like to be disturbed? Get him on the phone and tell him I wrote a damned good interview of him back in Chi years ago. Doesn't the guy have any gratitude?" With Bori standing behind him like Satan, Charlie kept talking until the lawyer agreed to call back. In five minutes, the phone rang and Charlie got the private number. In one more minute, Charlie actually got his party and was able to introduce Al Capone to Lucrezia Bori. Knowing Charlie, Capone was skeptical.

"How do I know who you are?" he asked Bori. "You could be some broad he's picked up."

He was beginning to sound cross and nobody wanted to make Al Capone cross.

"But, please Mr. Capone—I *am* Lucrezia Bori."

"Prove it," the gangster commanded.

Softly, Lucrezia started singing the drinking song from *La Traviata*.

A hush fell over the room and guests slowly drifted over to hear the treat.

Capone was convinced, and Mary's first birthday became history.

Bori, of course, was a great artist. She candidly told me that "Gatti-Casazza used to call me the Eskimo pie, because on the outside I am so sweet and delectable and then inside so ice cold." I found her anything but cold, though her whole life did center on singing. She had a dedication that was superhuman.

On the day of her appearances, she saw and spoke to no one. Once, when she had an operation for nodes on her vocal cord, she said not one word until she was healed weeks later. The slightest cough could have injured her voice permanently. Friends sat up with her in her villa in the south of France and played music and sang all night—three nights in a row, so she would not fall asleep and inadvertently cough. Her friends were terribly worried during this crisis and thought she might have lost her voice permanently. But Bori wasn't.

"I knew that my lover would come back," she said.

I was awed and suddenly despondent when I realized that my lover was my husband and, despite my conscientiousness, my work could never replace him. Now I was guilty about that. I certainly would never miss a performance if I could help it.

Charlie would ask, "Why must the show go on when you have a fever or your grandmother has just been shot by her lover? The audience will simply go home and play canasta."

Once, when I had a hundred and umpteen fever, Charlie put his foot down and took me to Doctors Hospital for a few days. My guilt about missing performances was somewhat relieved when, in my stupor, I lay listening to a playlet on the radio.

"Who owns that terrible, affected voice?" I asked, with the irritation of illness. "She's awful."

I almost didn't recover. I was listening to myself on some forgotten replay. I moaned and thought, *Perhaps I'm not robbing my public at all.*

I ceased being guilty—at least to the point where I eventually canceled Christmas Eve performances so I could be with my family.

* * *

It just didn't seem right not to be home Christmas Eve, planning the fun, wrapping the gifts. Charlie was adored by everybody because his only commitment was people. He lived on a dime, always ready to answer a call for help or companionship, which he considered synonymous.

The painter Giacometti said recently that if he had to save a Rembrandt canvas or a cat from a burning building, he would choose the cat because it was life. That was Charlie, whether it meant flirting with a rejected, ugly old hag, or lacing into Woollcott for sending a sleepy and mortified Will Durant to bed for not being a witty enough guest, or dropping everything to spend time with Scott Fitzgerald when Zelda had to be institutionalized. He was a magnet and they were all attracted to him like needles.

Scott stayed with us at our Manhattan flat for a few nights

to ease his depression. I can still see his lovely face when he told me that he had sentimentally given Zelda a bouquet of violets, which she promptly lifted to her ear.

"Do you hear what they're whispering, Scotty?" she had asked.

That was how he knew, once and for all, that it was hopeless. My heart went out to him, but of course I was working —I think it was in *Gilhooley*—and it was Charlie who never left his side. He drank with him and pulled him out of the black pit. It was true that when Charlie dragged him to see *Grand Hotel* their loudly voiced distaste for the production led to their being bodily removed; but at least Scott was feeling no pain and that was the whole idea.

Charlie MacArthur was a card, all right, the wildest in the deck—changeable and always welcome—the joker who could magically fill an inside straight for anyone but himself. To his whole era, he was good news, a day off, AWOL. But most of all—with his many gifts and his child's heart— Charlie was really Christmas. What a fool I would have been to miss the fun by working Christmas Eve.

As I look around my living room, I see a typical Christmas Past. It's like a dissolve in a sentimental film, but there they are: the half-hung garlands of green, the huge red satin bows, the fat sweet-smelling tree, and Charlie risking life and limb to hang the Angel Gabriel over the 18th-century crèche he'd found in Sorrento. The endless boxes and wrapping paper! The sound of our laughter still clings as we set the stage for this gayest of productions.

The children were asleep and their stockings hung from the mantel. Mary had decided that, with the weather this cold, we should leave Ovaltine and perhaps some cookies for Santa Claus. And so we had filled a Thermos for him before she retired.

Ruth Gordon was staying with us and worked as hard as we on the preparations.

"My God, the Ovaltine!" Ruth remembered, when we thought we'd finished. "We've got to get rid of it."

Charlie, the producer, swished the Ovaltine round in the cup, leaving a frothy lavender ring before he emptied the Thermos. He had not worked with the realistic Belasco for nothing. We then, under his direction, ate the cookies with a nightcap, leaving a telltale trail of crumbs from the tree to the fireplace. Under foot all night had been Caesar, one of the many dogs in our life. Charlie, noting the puppy's inordinate shyness at birth, had named him for the Roman general, hoping it would give him character. It never did. When everything was in its place, Charlie stole up on Caesar and yanked a sizeable hunk of white hair. Caesar retreated with a yowl. Charlie, unmoved, arranged the hair—supposedly from Santa's beard—on the cup.

"Now *that* is a stroke of genius," my husband modestly announced, taking a bow. And Ruth and I applauded him.

We were all so happy. We were all so young. I think, looking back, we all of us still believed in Santa Claus—all except Caesar, of course.

*   *   *

Our house was always filled with dogs, and still is. I can't think of a time in which their antics have not been part of our lives. They helped make our house a kennel, it is true, but the constant patter of their filthy paws and the dreadful results of their brainless activities have warmed me throughout the years. Charlie was a poodle man, himself, and introduced me to this most demented of species.

Sambo was our first and Charlie's greatest love. Sambo was long on charm and had no mind whatsoever. He had one talent: he ate felt hats. Since we didn't teach him any tricks he developed his own, which I suppose showed some initiative; but our male guests inevitably left more than their hearts with us. Sambo saw to that.

It was this stupid, charming, and vain dog that helped me create one of my favorite moments in the theatre. I fear that my characterization of the old Victoria, though based on Graddy Hayes, was part Sambo as well.

All poodles adore flattery, but to Sambo it was mothers' milk. You had only to croon, "Sambo, you are the most beautiful dog in the world," to drive him into a state of euphoria. His eyes would float heavenward, showing nothing but white crescents, and he would become fairly palsied with ecstasy.

The more unctuous the voice, the more flattering the words, the more intoxicated Sambo became. He was absolutely put into a trance; I've never seen anything so funny.

In the famous scene with Disraeli, in which the wily Prime Minister flatters Victoria outrageously in order to lure her out of an endless and unpopular period of mourning, I sat there like a candied apple—round and glazed and red-faced.

"Dizzy" was really going whole hog, and I was speechless, faced with this surfeit of praise.

I didn't move a muscle. Instead, I recalled Sambo.

I simply listened to Disraeli and felt myself getting drunk on his flattery, exactly as Sambo always had. Invariably—and it was incredible—someone in the audience would feel my intoxication and would titter. The amusement would then spread throughout the theatre and usually ended in applause.

Poor Sambo. He was a great dramatic teacher and such a fool. One night, when Charlie and I were walking him up in Nyack, he got mixed up with a skunk. We saw the striped animal just as Sambo did—under a street light—and tried desperately to divert his attention.

The dumbbell looked at us, and then made his decision.

It was his last. We covered him with a blanket and shipped him off to be de-skunked. He never returned: the medication they used on him proved fatal.

My last sight of him with that blanket wrapped around him, those sad eyes locked in last embrace with mine, made him look for all the world like Longfellow's Evangeline. It was a highly emotional scene, but then all poodles have theatre in their blood.

The first one I came to know well was Booth Tarkington's. That beautiful beast was a real ham. Mr. Tarkington's house in Indianapolis had a great sloping lawn that ended with a tall, spiked iron fence with a large gate. The author loved exercising the dog on the lawn and teaching him to perform in the cool of the early evening.

It took a little time for him to realize that the dog was listless and disinterested when there was no one about. When one person stopped at the gate and watched, the animal would perk up. As the spectators collected, he began performing with tremendous enthusiasm. By the time there was a crowd, he couldn't be removed from center stage.

Indeed, he went through his whole repertoire gladly— barking rhythmically, jumping over Mr. Tarkington's walking stick, fetching and carrying, and for the grand finale, ending with the *pièce de résistance*. A Black Republican, the author would loudly ask the poodle, "What ends would you go to rather than vote Democrat?"

The poodle now played dead.

There is just no tragedy as great as the self-pitying expression on a poodle's face when it is unhappy. The whole head seems to flatten with misery and it breaks my heart. Booth Tarkington was amused by it. In order to see the phenomenon, he would lift his finger and say, "Have you been a bad little dog today?" Or "Is there anything you're ashamed of?"

The poor poodle would fall apart, both body and spirit shattered. The top of that curly head flattened beyond recognition. I couldn't bear the sight, but now Mr. Tarkington would add, "Why don't you ask God to forgive you? You know He will," and the wretched beast, with hope in his heart, would place his paws over his face and kneel in supplication.

They are so wonderfully funny, poodles. I've never met a noble one and I am a dog-lover. When I hear tell of the character and the loyalty and devotion of dogs, I remain unmoved. All of my dogs have been scamps and thieves and troublemakers and I've adored them all. It's wonderful being loved unreservedly and even better being utterly depended on. And then, one can be so patronizing and always, always amused by their antics. Dogs have always enriched our household, and I wouldn't have had it any other way, for all the disasters they have caused.

*　*　*

It was Turvey the poodle with whom little Jamie had his Low Noon relationship. He came into our lives, stayed, and created a true dynasty. We were in San Francisco in 1939, trying out a play called *Ladies and Gentlemen* which Charlie and Ben Hecht had written for me. Charlie and I were at the Mark Hopkins, and in the elevator one evening we met a man whom Charlie recognized as the owner of the first short-haired fox terrier to win Best in Show at the Westminster Dog Show. The dog had actually made the cover of *Time* magazine that season. After Charlie congratulated the man, he was asked if we were interested in terriers.

"I'm a poodle man, myself," Charlie answered.

That was all this dog-lover had to hear. He knew where the best poodle in the world was—in England, at the Statter Kennels at Surrey. Since war seemed imminent, Miss Statter

—who ran the kennel and was concerned for the plight of all her dogs—was eager to find a good home for this, her favorite one.

Our producer, Gilbert Miller, had already suggested I go abroad with his wife, Kitty, in order to have Mainbocher do a wardrobe for me. So arrangements were immediately made for me to fetch this greatest of poodles, which had already won several blue ribbons and was now leading the life of a pampered stud.

We were in our second week in Paris, a time filled with fittings and shopping and party-going with Gilbert's pet notables, and we were dining at Lady Mendl's Villa Trianon near Versailles when Charlie called me from America.

"Will you get the hell out of there? Don't you know what's going to happen any second?"

"But Gilbert has his private plane and we can get to England easily," I blandly answered.

"Helen," Charlie went on, "every country has an actor who has a vendetta against a producer. Some lousy member of the *Luftwaffe* is going to be a frustrated Jedermann—an ex-actor with a grudge against Gilbert. Get the hell out *now!*"

I returned to the dinner table and heard my fellow guests making small talk about the crisis in Europe. Lady Mendl vowed that she was putting I.N.W. in the corner of all her invitations. Her eyes twinkled at our puzzlement. "If No War," she explained, chicly.

Only one man—a banker who told me he had removed a Rembrandt from his house and, with other possessions, had hidden them in a vault—was seriously aware.

Kitty and I arrived in Surrey, England, a day later. Gilbert's plane had been taken over by the government and all trucks and taxis had been commandeered as well. We arrived safely aboard a commercial plane. I wanted that dog, and Kitty and I got to Miss Statter's after booking passage on the *Champlain* sailing from Southhampton.

When we got out of the car that afternoon, Kitty, more chic than ever in a black Mainbocher, was chased through the brush by a flock of geese nipping at her heels. It was a mad sight, and comical but for our sudden feeling that it might be an omen. The goose step was crossing the Continent and threatening England. Charlie was righter than ever.

We grabbed the dog named Turvey and drove straight to the ship, over the bumpiest of roads, attempting to console this frightened, wretched animal. He was so beautiful, with a great mane and ruffs at his ankles, his circus cut anything but gay. The dog had been torn from his beloved Miss Statter and was in a trauma. By the time we reached the dock and waited to board ship, I realized I was going to have a problem.

Gaily decorated with a big red bow, Turvey should have been in black crepe. He was in a deep depression.

I was soon to discover that the 1300 other passengers were as grateful as Charlie that we were all on our way to America. Many Poles were aboard, and their fear communicated itself to others momentarily less involved with the Germans. Those 11 days on the blacked-out ship were filled with terror and tales of experiences that preceded the embarkation. Word reached us that the *Athenia* had been torpedoed. We pursued our zigzag course across the Atlantic sealed up in complete darkness every night. The boat was jammed, but after the first day the sheer relief of being en route lifted everyone's spirits.

Turvey remained morose. More than that, he remained nonfunctioning. On the third day, I was really worried. He had neither eaten nor relieved himself.

The hunger strike was one thing, but his unwillingness to unburden his grief was something else again. I cajoled and walked him, implored him and walked him, offered him all manner of delicacies and walked him. The days kept passing as he became more and more emaciated. It was heartbreaking.

When we returned to my small cabin, he would hide under the bed and refuse to emerge. When I got down on the floor and lifted the bedcover, I saw his amber eyes staring at me in misery. Afraid to put my hand under the bed for fear I might lose it, I just lay there trying to reason with him. On the fifth day of his fast, I dragged him up to the deck and walked him again. He barely had the strength, poor darling.

This is the dog Charlie wants, I thought bitterly. He *won't survive the crossing. He'll just die of starvation or burst of uremic poisoning.*

I had discussed this problem with everyone on the ship and nobody could make the smallest suggestion. It was just awful. As I lay on my deck chair staring at him, his glazed eyes avoided mine always by a hair's breadth. He just wouldn't respond.

I shook my head philosophically and looked away. There on the deck near my chair was a quoit that someone had left. I idly threw it back to the court. Turvey heaved a great sigh and rose to retrieve it. He returned with the green quoit hanging from his mouth and looked for all the world like a door-knocker.

"Why, thank you, Turvey!" I took the quoit and threw it again. Once more, the dog fetched and retrieved. Again and again, and then he walked with great dignity to a pile of ropes near the rail. As my fellow passengers watched him sadly, he lifted his leg.

In all my born days, I never saw the like of that performance. It lasted for fully five minutes. People were screaming, "Bravo!" "C'est formidable!" and making book on the time. Turvey had held out, but now he was released. The pressure was gone and Turvey returned to normal, and became so possessive that he was like a jealous lover.

Back in Nyack, he would howl outside our bedroom door, a one-man shivaree. He was outside because he knew what went on inside and had been exiled. All Charlie had to do was put his arm around me and Turvey went for the seat of his pants.

"Dammit, that dog is inhibiting me."

It became a feud.

I'm afraid that Turvey's adoration of me was almost obscene. I couldn't be out of his sight. One night I went up the road to visit the Hechts, and left Turvey at home. He made a dog-shaped hole in a window screen in order to follow me. It was just like a prop in a vaudeville act. He would follow me everywhere except into the pool, which frightened him—so he ruined every dive as he disapprovingly took a playful nip at me as I took off. Turvey was impossible.

During the run of *Harriet*, I dropped him off one matinee day to be groomed and coiffed. This is really important for poodles who, allowed to go without a haircut, start to sweep the ground with matted hair like yaks. It causes them embarrassment. When they return from beauty shops they become gloriously comic and comically vainglorious. Those pompoms on their hips, the ruffs at the ankles, the crown of curls! When Turvey was delivered to the Henry Miller Theater that day, he was divine—Charles II in a particularly festive mood.

The maid Priscilla was cautioned to keep him tied up in my dressing room, so that he couldn't follow me on stage, but Turvey always frightened Priscilla. Probably it was just his great size. What happened I will never know—except that crazy, love-mad Turvey broke loose and set out to find me.

It was a warm spring night and that is probably how the dressing-room door happened to be open. But so was the alley door. Once in the corridor, over-civilized Turvey lost my scent. I had gone left to the stage, he went right—right outside the theatre to 43rd Street. White-uniformed Priscilla was in frantic pursuit, of course, but she was heavy and not fleet. She was both duck-seated and -footed. It must have been a spectacle.

"Help, stop the dog!" she shouted as the red-bowed animal sprinted up the street, the head of a parade. Behind Priscilla were two actors who played my brothers, the Beechers in the play. Dressed in Prince Albert frock coats and beards, they wouldn't even be noticed today, when a whole role-playing generation seems intent on making every day Mardi Gras. But in 1941 only professional actors walked around in costume.

The chase went on until, in some surprising atavism, Turvey disappeared among the trees of Bryant Park on 42nd Street adjoining the Public Library. Priscilla, disillusioned with humanity—not one person in the street tried to help her—"They just stood there staring" she reported—gave up the chase, and the actors raced back to the theatre breathlessly to pick up their cues. Then the shock set in for all of us. Turvey was swallowed up in the greatest metropolis in the world, a helpless beautiful fool.

Charlie and I did not go back to Nyack that night. We stayed in town, in constant touch with the police. Terrible tales of dog-napping drove me to distraction. Suggestions that we call the pound and the city dump, my horror at remembering Irene Castle McLaughlin's stories of vivisection on those poor demented lost things, and Priscilla's tears all persuaded me that Turvey was already decimated.

Charlie tried to convince me that no one would send such a magnificent animal to the pound, but I couldn't be sure of anything. It was a sleepless night at the Algonquin Hotel, and along about eight A.M. the police called. Turvey had been found. He was discovered at the *New York Times* Building on Times Square. He was in a telephone booth.

I fell back in relief. Charlie sighed and shook his head.

"The poor devil. He obviously didn't have a nickel."

Turvey! He loved not wisely but too well. As flattering as it was, there were times when I thought I would go stark raving mad. I was his prime interest, his mania, his life.

When I was on tour with a play, Turvey was left with Mary and Jamie. Despite their spate of governesses, I used to fly back home for weekends to see them. When I didn't, my remorse and loneliness were worse than the fatigue. I remember doing some television show years later, a commitment I couldn't avoid, when there was a birthday party at home for which I was going to be late. Mildred Dunnock, with whom I was working, asked what was wrong, my face was so long, my air so preoccupied.

When I told her, she said only, "So you live in a guilt box, too!"

So much for the glamorous life of actresses.

But I digress. Back to Turvey, about whom I felt no guilt whatsoever.

In the midst of a blizzard at 6 A.M., we arrived in Rochester during the *Victoria* tour. I really needed some hot coffee before I went to bed. It was too early for room service—but I was directed to the closed nightclub downstairs, where they unstacked a table and chair and warmed up last night's coffee for me. As I enjoyed the life of a star, a letter was brought to me.

It was from Alec Woollcott, the self-apointed Toscanini who had to conduct everything from no matter what distance.

"Dear Helen," it began, "you have got—as a matter of fact, I *command* you—to send for Turvey. The dog is languishing without you. He'd rather be locked in a train on a railroad siding with you than be without you in that forest of trees. He's *pining* away. . . ."

Slowly my weary brain absorbed what I was reading. Then there stirred within me not remorse, but crazy, ecstatic triumph. I was here, Turvey was there, and I didn't have to walk him around the block in this blizzard. Poor Alec! He was such a sentimentalist.

His own poodle, Pip—or, as he and Dickens called the leading character in *Great Expectations*, "Dear Boy"—was the bachelor's closest chum. A most literary and intellectual dog, to be sure, and as precious as one would expect a Woollcott pet to be.

Dear Boy had a collection of toys and props with which he used to show off when there was company. After this usually unsolicited performance, he would replace each prop neatly. He was like some horrible child who curtsies constantly, never raises her voice, and is absolutely immaculate, nary a toy or hair out of place. Like Theodore Roosevelt Jr.'s poodle, Poilu, Dear Boy was a true elegant with a pride and dignity our poodles never had. I always thought Dear Boy a bore and so, obviously, did Turvey.

Alec never invited us to Wit's End, his country place on Lake Bomoseen. He would order us there for the weekend. Charlie called those visits Jury Duty. This particular time, Alec insisted that we bring Turvey so that he and Dear Boy could keep each other company. We begged him to let the dog off the hook.

"Dear Boy will find Turvey insufferable, Alec. You know

how elegant he is," Charlie said. "Turvey can be an awful boor."

"Enough!" Alec answered. "He is a dear, loving beast and I find this character assassination appalling. Why indeed do you have a pet if you think so little of him? No! I insist he come. Why shouldn't *he* enjoy the wonders of my place and, incidentally, the stimulation of my company? He has always shown a penchant for the civilized. He likes me. He will like my dog."

"It's on your head, Maestro," Charlie answered, rather hoping it would be much lower.

Turvey greeted Alec with all the love in him, but he immediately banished Dear Boy to the kitchen for the entire weekend. Once competition was out of the way, Turvey took over and flattered his host with much attention. He was a superb beast and simply abided Dear Boy as long as he didn't mix with the guests. It was the same proprietary manner with which he accepted Charlie, as long as he didn't appropriate me.

One day, in true annoyance, Charlie insanely thumbed his nose at the dog. I never saw anything in my life like Turvey's outrage. He went into a real state. Obviously, he knew an insult when he saw one. In some curious way, he understood the gesture. Charlie had learned how to get even with his rival. He simply thumbed his nose at the dog and Turvey went crazy—barking, howling, jumping around literally beside himself. Charlie won that round, but not the fight.

*   *   *

Turvey had a wife we had arranged for him. Her name was Canaille, which Charlie suggested because it was French for riffraff. He thought the name fit her. Through

Canaille, Turvey sired nine pups which were, in turn, to keep his descendents in our house until 1965. That first litter was incredible. They hung from Turvey's ears, tail, dewlaps, and genitalia. His long-suffering acceptance of those indignities led my husband to observe, "Boy, is that son of a so-and-so paying for his pleasures."

From one of their litters came the beauteous Camille. She was as white as Turvey was black and became Mary's special pup, attaching herself to the child as her father did me. Everywhere that Mary went that pup was sure to follow. Inheriting her father's resourcefulness, as well as his capacity for suffocating love, Camille was a canine Houdini. There wasn't a pen that could hold her, a door or window that could separate her from her love.

One day I heard a taxi pull up in our drive way. It was nine A.M., and I wondered who could be calling at such an hour. I looked out the window and saw the driver get out and open the door. Out stepped Camille, his sole fare. She had followed Mary to school and had been placed in the cab and shipped home in a style to which, I'm afraid, she became accustomed.

During the war, Camille got herself *enceinte* and was about to have her litter when I was off to Washington to meet Charlie. He had just joined the Army and, for the nonce, was stationed there. Mary couldn't come with me because, as she put it, "My place is with my dog." Mary was twelve and I had doubts about leaving her, but Guy Monneypenny, a dear friend and actor momentarily at liberty, promised to watch over things.

Mary called on Saturday in high excitement.

"She's starting, Mommy. Camille is starting, I can tell, and Guy's gotten sick, but I have everything under control and everything's just fine."

"What are you doing for her, Mary?"

"I've put a pot of water on to boil," she answered.

"What are you going to do with it?"

"I haven't figured it out yet but that's what they do in the movies whenever someone's having a baby."

Mary was right about Camille's starting. It was a long delivery and she kept us informed every half hour.

"Oh, Mommy, she's had another one and it's *so* cute."

"Oh, Mommy, this one's white and—darling!"

When Camille had reached seven, I observed that perhaps her dog was overdoing it a bit and Mary couldn't have agreed more.

"I keep waiting for her to stop, but I think it's beyond her control."

Camille stopped when she was good and ready. This was Mary's last bulletin and she was absolutely in triumph.

"There are nine puppies, Mommy, and they're all eating and I used the boiling water to make tea for Guy and he feels much better."

Motherhood did nothing to mature Camille. She was as wayward as her father and a good deal more aggressive about it. Her inclination to chase anyone who passed our property at seven A.M. caused us no end of trouble. It was really just mischief, but the workmen, servants, and civil employees off to their jobs were not in the least charmed. Camille went for ladies' stockings and gentlemen's pants. The complaints started to pile up and we thought seriously about having an apology printed up for all occasions.

The situation became serio-comic when our local pharmacist, Mr. Nathanson, wrote us a letter fraught with implications. "First my mother," it began ominously, "then my brother, and now me. What next?" it ended darkly.

I really believe that the Nathansons suspected us of being

anti-Semites who had directed their mastiff to stop them from passing our house. I could only explain the MacArthur position. Charlie, already actively anti-Nazi, was so furious that he rolled up the morning newspaper that told of Hitler's sweep through Europe, and whacked Camille with it.

"That," Charlie shouted, "is for the Nathansons."

But Camille was not prejudiced. She went for everybody and we were helpless. Mary adored her so. We reached a point of such distress that we considered getting rid of her, but our gardener, Freddie, joined forces with Mary. His plea for mercy was eloquent.

"She no a bite people, Mrs. MacArthur. She jus' a run into them with her mouth open."

It was quite a state of affairs, with Mary terrified that she would come home from school and find her beloved gone and the rest of Nyack praying that the beast be made into mincemeat.

Obviously, this was the time for decisive action, and, after a great deal of investigation, I discovered a lady in New York who had just cured Walter Lippman's dog of a like problem. A dog psychologist, the lady wrote for the *New York Times* and ran an obedience school. I would spare no expense in order to bring peace back to the streets of Nyack. The first step was to have dog and lady meet.

"We'll fix her up in a wink," the good lady announced heartily, after the first interview at our house, as she smiled at cuckoo but suspicious Camille in order to ingratiate herself. And then she outlined her plan.

"Mrs. MacArthur," she began, "it is the simplest of gambits. The problem is as good as solved. Believe me, this isn't the first mad poodle I will have cured! Now then, it is most important that you rise one hour before the trouble and hide in the shrubbery—"

"Hide in the shrubbery?"

"Of course, at the scene of the crimes. You will be holding a BB gun—with paper pellets, of course. . . ."

"Of course," I agreed, dumbfounded. "Paper pellets."

"These pellets will only sting her body but shatter her pride. Now you must be there an hour before she is let out so that your scent will be gone. When Camille attacks a passerby, you will jump out of the bushes, make a great noise as you shoot the BB gun. Your dog will *never* want to relive this trauma."

I listened patiently. Returning to Nyack after a performance on Broadway, I never got to sleep until, at least, one o'clock in the morning. I couldn't see myself greeting the dawn—soaking wet in the dew, scratched, and shivering with cold as I hid in the bushes.

"Very interesting," I said dumbly. "But aren't you leaving something out? In the first place, I am not a sharpshooter and how do I explain to the judge why I have been armed and lurking in the bushes to shoot old charladies at seven o'clock in the morning because that's who's going to get shot, you know, not the demented beast."

I was not being very cooperative and the lady moved up to Nyack to perform the task herself. Every morning at six, she hid in the bushes, and every morning at seven, Camille loped across the lawn and aimed straight for the shrubbery, where she would join the huntress. As long as the lady was there, Camille refused to attack a soul. It was really terrible. We could hardly employ the woman for the rest of Camille's life.

After much musing and re-evaluation, there was a change in the lady's plan. "I will just have to wait *inside* the house and, at the moment of Camille's attack, I will dash out, shocking her into docility."

With an automobile snow chain, this dedicated woman would emerge like an Indian each morning, hollering and whooping as she threw the clanging chain at the dog. Camille thought she was playing a game and began luring her new companion, obviously looking forward to the scene—which, incidentally, woke the whole house.

Camille was wearing her down, and Madam Psychologist was becoming a trifle wild-eyed. She started hiring little boys to run by the driveway to encourage the attacks to which she was going to put an end, but Camille would have none of them. She far preferred our house guest and her endless games. Walter Lippman's dog may have been cured. Mine was not. Admitting defeat and no doubt by that time somewhat rheumatic, the lady left, and Camille immediately attacked Judge Patterson the very next morning. Judge Patterson, whose bench was our county court in New York City, didn't have much of his trousers left.

The judge was a kind man. He observed that he would need new trousers and he made no official complaint, but he exacted payment nonetheless. He asked if I would join him in a ceremony in which he was swearing in a hundred foreigners as American citizens. I ended the ceremony with a recital of *America*. I was all dignity—Columbia herself— and only the judge knew I was really getting myself off the hook because of that nut Camille.

❄ ❄ ❄

Camille was Turvey's daughter, and that made stuffy me consider any romance between them shocking. I just can't get myself to allow a papa dog to mate with his own off- spring. When Camille came into heat, she drove Turvey mad. He became possessed with her and I had to separate them. It was the day before Charlie was returning from the Sec- ond War with his little bag of emeralds. Turvey had switched his devotion from me to Camille; though I was relieved, I could not accept this incestuous business.

That night poor Turvey, robbed of his love, was so disturbed that he sat in the hall and wailed all night like a banshee. It was just awful. His grief was as Grecian as his appetite. That wail was an echo of ancient tragedy.

Charlie was home the next day and in my happy excitement I forgot about Turvey's problem. But that night he was worse.

"I have come home from the war to *this!*" Charlie said.

"Woooooooooooo!" Turvey responded.

"Damn it. You're my wife."

"It's not for me this time, Charlie. It's for Camille. The darned fool wants Camille and I can't—I just can't. . . ."

"I will not spend another night in this house with that going on. It's like the *Hound of the Baskervilles.*"

In the morning, Charlie called the vet and explained the situation. The vet simply suggested that we calm him down with some saltpeter. The next morning, I walked into town to go to the drugstore. When I entered, a few of the town's ladies were shopping and chatting with Mrs. Shea, the druggist's wife. The president of the garden club, with a huge pompadour and little hat, spoke first.

"We're so glad for you, Mrs. MacArthur. We hear that the colonel returned last night."

"Yes," I answered happily.

"How is charming Colonel MacArthur? Please send him our best."

"Very well—he's never been better. Fit as a fiddle!"

"How you must have missed each other. Thank heavens he's back safely."

As the ladies congratulated me, Mrs. Shea asked if she could be of any service.

"Yes, Mrs. Shea. I'd like some saltpeter."

Blissfully ignorant me. I didn't realize what made the club ladies fall so silent. Only later did I realize what made that pompadour rise even higher.

"How much do you want, Mrs. MacArthur?" Mrs. Shea continued shyly.

And then I said it—the thing that made Charlie rage more than anything else.

"As much as you would give Turvey!"

It wasn't until my walk home, my package safely in hand, that it occurred to me. My mouth opened in shock. It was the slowest take of my career. It started with a soft chuckle and by the time I arrived home I was shaking with laughter. It was actually painful and I staggered into the house, sputtering, "You'll never believe what I've done—Charlie— oh, Charlie."

When I was at last able to relate the story, Charlie threw his hands up.

"That damned dog has done me in again."

Turvey was Charlie's nemesis. No doubt about that. He gave him no quarter, right up to the bitter end. And the end came when Turvey was 15. He had a long and insane life and he died of joy, Turvey did.

His happiness was boundless. Whenever it was time to go out and he saw me reach for his leash, he would jump with joy and then make a beeline for the hallway, where he would go into his mad capers.

On the last night, he darted down the hall and fell over, unconscious. My heart sank, but Charlie refused to believe it was over. He called the vet while I sat sobbing, with Turvey's curly head in my lap. It was impossible to find a vet that night. They were all at a banquet at the Commodore Hotel in New York. But Charlie wouldn't be daunted. Their crazy relationship was a close one, their silly enmity a constant in this most fickle of worlds.

I can still see my Charlie tenderly holding that immense animal in his arms as he carried him off to the Ellen Speyer Hospital.

Turvey was dead by the time we got there. They gave us his collar and we walked back to the waiting taxi, absolutely crushed. Charlie put his arm around me without interference. Their feud was over now.

"He had a long and happy life, Helen," Charlie began. He pulled the front of his jacket round and there were tears in his eyes.

"Well, anyway, he's had the last word again."

"What do you mean, Darling?" I asked.

Charlie said, "I'm soaking wet."

13

Nᴏᴛ long ago, when Jim got a new German Shepherd for his children, he named it Timmy. I was disappointed, thinking it hardly descriptive or dignified enough.

"But don't you remember, Mom?" he asked, still round-eyed. "You mean you don't remember Timochenko? My pal Timmy?"

Then I was reminded. When I did *Glass Menagerie* at the Haymarket in London after the war, Jamie stayed with me at Bea Lillie's Park Lane flat while Charlie took Mary on a grand tour of the Continent. He was about ten at the time and used to play pitchpenny backstage and then watch the show—every performance. He knew the part of Tom perfectly and once played it for me in the dressing room immediately displaying the instincts of a real actor.

Coming events were casting their shadows—but Jamie was still a little boy. Daily, he stopped in front of the Dorchester Hotel where he had met a shepherd dog. It belonged to Jim Donovan, the foreign correspondent, who had named the animal after the Russian hero.

Boy and dog became fast friends, and Jamie looked forward to their daily encounters as the high point of his stay. The shepherd would sit with the doorman, his serious face turned east, his brow wrinkled with impatience, his eyes glued to the corner around which the object of his devotion —my son—would suddenly appear. Both of these love-besotted creatures would then break away and run toward each other, like Jeannette MacDonald and Nelson Eddy at the technicolored end of one of their confections.

Mary, on the last lap of her holiday, wanted to show Jamie Paris and begged me to send him over. She had to share with him the wonders of that beautiful city. She and Charlie took him to the Bois and the Punch and Judy show and the Eiffel Tower. Despite his joy at being with Mary and his father his heart was back in London. Not with Mom, but with Timmy.

The shepherd in turn was languishing in front of the Dorchester in a reverie. His devotion had made him a catatonic. He just sat—a slight twitch his only activity—staring at Jamie's corner. And across the Channel, Jamie suffered all the pleasures of Paris, like a lover brought to Europe by his family to forget.

He was the specter at the feast. Everywhere he went, little Jamie saw only the drooling, tail-wagging Timmy, sitting like Mexico's Empress Carlotta, waiting.

Twenty years had passed and Jim had remembered his chum and given still another child—his own Charlie—a Timmy to play with, another thing to love.

❖   ❖   ❖

In this world, where we keep hearing about the problems of communication and the inability to feel and relate, my son is blessedly out of step. And I think it all goes back to Mary. When we brought the infant Jamie home, we told Mary that we had looked far and wide for the very best of brothers and that he was hers.

She took us at our word. Mary, the old soul, accepted that imp on his own terms as no one else could. She cherished and fought for her brother whenever Charlie or I decided that murder was the only solution to our problem. There were those lumbering noises that filled our houses like an army, and Mary was the darling of our A.E.F. Her unflinching affection and loyalty earned her his abject love.

Mary had first appeared on stage with me in *Alice Sit By the Fire* in Olney, Maryland, and the next season she was invited by Richard Skinner to be the company ingenue. While rehearsing in *The Corn Is Green* with Frances Starr, she called and asked if Jim could come down and be one of the miner's children in the play, so he could spend the summer with her.

"It'll be such fun having him here, all smudged-up and Welsh and everything, and you know I'll take care of him, Mom."

Mary was too light-hearted and playful to be embarrassingly noble. She was never conscious of being "good." Frankly, I was always astonished at her lack of guile and pretext. As a popular 16-year-old, always on the phone, she never revealed by the tone of her voice whether she was talking to a boy or a girl. It would never have occurred to her to put on a performance. Her mother has never been without an awareness of herself. I admit this readily.

When Mary was about four and I was playing *Victoria Regina*, I affected lorgnettes for a while. Whenever I had to read anything, I would lift them to my eyes momentarily and then allow them to fall safely on my proud bosom. Little did I know that I had bred a critic in my very own house. One night, before sleep, this angelic baby was praying unintelligibly. She was babbling her prayers, making them sound like the jabberwocky she loved so much. It was simply a gesture, and a sloppy one at that. I shook my head gravely. "I *think* of God when *I* pray, Darling," I said, as I leaned over the bed. My voice couldn't have been more patronizing and my lorgnettes hung over her face. She now put them to her eyes and imitated my tone.

"I *see* God," she said. "He has a big white beard and a cold in his nose."

She was a great de-bunker, my Mary, and had an alarming grasp on truth. I think her serenity and poise were the result of her innocence. There was never any conflict or dissembling. Her reactions were immediate and pure. Kent Smith said that he had never met a human being so perfectly adjusted.

When the Nyack High School was planning two basketball teams—one Negro and one white in order to enforce segregation—she was calmly furious and started a successful crusade to stop such nonsense by petitioning all the students.

"It's true they're better, Mommy, and it might serve us right to have it proven; but I just can't bear the idea of separate teams."

Just five years later, at the same time that Washington's National Theater closed rather than accept Negroes in the orchestra, Mary and I proudly appeared in the first desegregated theatre in the South, where we did *Alice Sit by the Fire*. Only one couple moved in protest.

❋   ❋   ❋

Mary was a born pro, so of course she was nervous on her debut. But like her father—so much like her father—she couldn't take anything about herself too seriously. They were both always slightly bewitched, strangely detached, for all their passion for justice and talent for loving.

No matter what was going on—even during crises—they both were possessors of a delightful secret. Always, there was the slight twitch at the corners of the mouth and the tiny gleam hiding in the eyes. My husband and daughter shared the knowledge of something that caused them to live on the edge of laughter, barely able to contain themselves. They were of a radiant piece, those two.

Mary giggled all through the rehearsals with Josh Logan, who bought a BB gun and threatened her with it. She roared, but on opening night she put her hands to her face in our dressing room.

"Mommy, I'm getting scared."

"Well, don't," I sympathized.

And she was fine.

When I was about to open in *Happy Birthday*, I was a wreck and visiting Mary sat calm and cool as a cucumber, watching me dress and comforting me.

"Now you know you'll be perfect, Mommy."

I looked at her through the mirror.

"This isn't just my plain, old-fashioned stage fright, Mary. *That* I can handle. But I have to do that blasted dance and I'm going to fall right on my face. Now talk me out of that if you can. What happens when I fall right on my face?"

I can see her smile right this moment.

"So what happens is that 'you pick yourself up, dust yourself off, and start all over again.' It won't be the end of the world."

We both laughed.

Three years later, those words returned to me. That Mary could help me, even about her own death, was typical and marvelous.

The night of her debut in *Alice Sit By the Fire*, I was so nervous that I fluffed a line and *Mary* covered *me*. Charlie sat in the audience, first frightened for Mary and then almost sinfully proud. He couldn't have borne it, were she not talented. No fear! Backstage, he presented her with a bunch of violets, a single red rose in its center. He had brought her the identical bouquet the day she was born, on their very first date, and it always remained his Valentine.

❋   ❋   ❋

Mary was Charlie's creation, his most precious possession. After her River Club coming-out party, she began to go out a great deal. Pretty and gay, already irrevocably part of the theatre, she now struck Charlie as the potential victim of all predatory males.

Unconventional Charlie MacArthur, the maverick, now became the most traditional of fathers and worse—Cotton Mather. Exactly on cue, he became suspicious and overprotective. The thought of all those "grubby quarterbacks" touching his vestal daughter terrified him. He was in perpetual panic that her beauty and purity would be despoiled by the goats and minotaurs—whom everyone else saw as wholesome, crew-cut Ivy undergraduates, or dreamy, idealistic fellow actors.

Like St. George, Charlie stood ready to kill any dragonet, exhaling his first cigarette smoke through his burning nostrils.

"Do you have any trouble, Mary? I mean—and you know darn well what I mean—do you have to defend yourself against these downy, hot-blooded hooligans?"

"Who doesn't, Pop?" Mary answered.

"I don't, dammit!" he exploded, half wishing she weren't so honest.

"I'm O.K., Pop," she now comforted him, "I've worked out something that's foolproof."

"You have?"

"Of course. When I'm going to be alone with a boy in a cab or anywhere I toss some gum in my mouth. Then when I see a lunge coming, I just blow a big bubble and it kills the whole mood."

Charlie was stunned rather than relieved, and he reverted to type immediately.

"But a fellow can be marked for the rest of his life by that great, revolting, pink thing billowing out of a girl's mouth!"

He was suddenly all sympathy for Mary's dates.

"The poor bastards," was his final observation.

Mary was her father's daughter, and how lucky she was to have him as a father.

He took her to Europe and gave her the Grand Tour as only Charlie could. I know. In 1938 he was certain it was the eve of disaster and wanted us to share Europe before it disappeared. Through his eyes I was able to fix forever all that was beautiful in that world.

The war came and went. And then, our daughter was lucky enough to enjoy the remaining drops of those surviving vineyards with a perfect companion. With Charlie she was welcomed everywhere the beautiful and accomplished reigned. This was Charlie's old playground, and where he held court. It was only proper and fitting that his princess, Mary, be presented and given the royal treatment. He took her everywhere and she met everyone.

They glided through the Continent—Capri, Rome, Paris, Antibes, St. Moritz, everywhere—and she had as escorts Tyrone Power, Orson Welles, princes and social lions. All the dazzlers were there, and Charlie saw to it that she missed no one, from his favorite bartender to Pope Pius.

"I want our Mary to have every experience," he wrote me.

Charlie's friends were legion. He could have been dropped by helicopter into the Antarctic and there surely would have been a few hard-drinking, quick-witted Eskimos he had picked up somewhere along the line who adored him and made their igloos his. It was inevitable that my eclectic husband would have friends in the Vatican, through whom he met the Vicar of St. Peter's. The Vicar was an American monsignor who lived on the top floor of a Roman palazzo and loved bourbon. Mary and Charlie carried a case of Kentucky up four flights to the priest's apartment.

"Is God in?" Charlie inquired, as he knocked on the door.

I have never had one one moment's doubt, despite those years during which I lost grace—but Charlie understood the ache beneath my joyous life with him, and he always felt remorse.

There in the Eternal City, throwing himself enthusiastically into the Roman scene and, no doubt, sharing his gift with the good monsignor, Charlie called me in New York and offered to become a Catholic if this would help me return to the fold, ending my painful exile. His heart was in the right place, and the pageantry of the Church was doubtless intoxicating; but I would not allow him to do it.

That was not my road back to Rome.

* * *

Mary and I were appearing together in *Good Housekeeping* up at Westport, Connecticut, when she caught the cold that turned out to be polio. Her fatigue seemed excessive and I sent her home to Nyack against her will.

Charlie was at the Lenox Hill Hospital being treated for his ulcers, and a few days after her return she joined him across the hall—still insisting that I stay with the play and open in Bucks County, where she would then rejoin me.

Charlie, at first agreeing with her, now called me when

the doctor became suspicious. I closed the play and rushed to New York, where I found Mary in an iron lung.

"Open those beautiful brown eyes," the doctor coaxed her when I arrived.

"Blue!" Charlie muttered agressively, as he squeezed my hand.

It isn't reasonable to outlive one's child. It is against everything natural, but it happens. It happened to us. Our Mary lost her battle a few days later. She was 19.

When Miss Fleming brought Jamie into town, he was bewildered. His loss was as great as ours and I think as time went on he had an extra burden to carry. We were helpless to lighten it, no matter how we tried. Charlie and I could only try to prove our love for him, ceaselessly.

"Your mother and I are going to need you even more now —need you to take care of us," Charlie said to the sobbing child.

That little boy took a manly stab at it. He touched my hand.

"You know, Mom—up in Nyack they're taking up the trees and there's going to be a ball game and—and—you'll enjoy it."

Our tragedy was mutual and we mourned as a family— holding hands in the ritual pavan; but such anguish, like ecstacy, is divisive and I fear that each of us, one insulated from the other, stood alone and irreparably altered.

As for Brownie, who was herself in the hospital at this time, it was the beginning of the end.

* * *

Charlie became stronger than he had ever been when he saw me sway. He became my bastion until I regained my balance. When I did, he stumbled—never to right himself again. He had rallied for me and this last, great burst of energy was too much for his sick body and tired soul.

He now started his tragic pursuit of the blithe spirit who was our daughter. His decline was slow, but steady—his holidays from reality more extended, his periods of productivity dwindling simply to talk. His powers were ebbing and I watched my husband grow old before my eyes: not imperceptibly, so that one day you say of some unchanging friend, in a moment of illumination, "Heavens, when did he become old?"; but, rather, overnight—in a shocking dissolve.

We never seemed to be strong together—at the same time —except when we were fresh in love and fighting the forces that would have kept us apart. For that, I will always be grateful. How terrible it would have been to have missed my life with him.

As battles are lost and wars still won, there were admittedly regrettable moments in my marriage, but they do not alter the larger truth. Charlie MacArthur and I had found each other in the crowd—he never stopped calling me his bride. That miracle remains.

When Mary was born and my dreams and plans knew no horizon, Charlie, my Scottish gypsy, smiled sadly.

"We have given her life and death, Helen. That's all we can be sure of."

And now Charlie started dying, when he was certain that I would survive.

I visited Mary's grave one winter's day recently, with a birthday bouquet of her favorite flowers. They had been her first present from a gentleman, that bouquet she'd received the first day of her life from her father.

When I arrived at the cemetery, I found that a recent snow had left such drifts that the path to Mary was impassable. After circling the area and testing the crustiness of the snow's surface, I could only give up after landing knee-deep in one of the shallower approaches.

Terribly disappointed, I looked at the bunch of violets that circled the one red rose and refused to be daunted. They were for Mary and, by gum, Mary was going to have them. Taking careful aim, I pitched the flowers across the great drift and they landed—a brilliant explosion of color—on the frozen grave. *Daddy would have been proud of me*, I thought. It was a pitch worthy of Walter Johnson.

The absurdity of the moment would have delighted Mary. I knew that. It suddenly struck me funny as well. It was the first laugh my daughter and I shared in many years, and I was refreshed by it.

*　*　*

It might at first have been anger that made me dedicate myself to the National Foundation and its crusade to wipe out Polio. But then I met one of the medical heads whose own children had been afflicted and who was determined to see that others would not be.

I was struck by the fact that, if there is any divinity, it is in man's willingness to help alleviate suffering in others. We are all too familiar with man's venality. It is highly publicized and even admired; but there is man's nobility, too. I knew without the slightest doubt that Mary could continue to help cheer others, and I knew that this would please her happy spirit.

"I will not let Mary be used as a tambourine!" Charlie exclaimed. But this time he was wrong, and he came to realize it.

Starting with the Mary MacArthur Fund, which some of Mary's theatre friends had created in her memory and to which the entire theatre responded so generously, a 12-bed respiratory ward at Wellesley Center, in Boston's Children's Hospital, was made possible. This proved a training ground for many of the great doctors who had to learn their special craft. Much of their work radiated from this center until Jonas Salk licked the killer once and for all.

Once Dr. Salk had the blessed vaccine and had overcome the dread microbe, he had to conquer the public's fear of inoculation. Shades of Brownie back in Washington, another life ago. I remembered Mother's early prejudice against vaccination and found myself working with frightened children and suspicious parents. I felt I was doing re-takes for Sinclair Lewis's *Arrowsmith*, which I had filmed years before. I gratefully was able to throw myself into constructive activity and the work I did allowed me release, carrying me over the abyss, back to the land of the living. Being needed saved my sanity. Then the theatre, as always, came to my rescue.

At home, the man who had lighted the brightest of salons sat in gloom. Like Hamlet, he was suffering the slings and arrows of outrageous fortune. Sickness and drink were taking their toll, but the blow he had just been dealt was the fatal one.

Long after his youth was past, Charlie and his friends had stubbornly played at being boys. Now his youth had been snatched from him by his daughter's death. He could no longer pretend.

Charlie was not meant to grow old, and he quite evidently decided not to.

"I don't mind going," Charlie said, in the hospital. "I believe in God, Helen, and I'm not afraid. It's just this lousy exit they've written for me."

My career was through when Charlie died. It had been

important to him throughout the years, and to the children. Sometimes I think I was just showing off for them—to make them proud of me.

There are those who believe that people who have been mortally wounded should be lifted to their feet immediately and returned to action. In the world of doers that I lived in, that's the way things should be. So my close friends, headed by Anita Loos and Lillian Gish, urged me to play in *Anastasia* with Ingrid Bergman.

One has to protect oneself from the earnest friends who would help you in adversity. They were too much for me and I relented—not wanting to be a burden to anyone, especially Jim. Work had always helped me before.

And so I returned. But this time I needed more than the protection of the theater. I needed more than work. For over 30 years, no matter what else was ever wrong, I had had Charlie. Now I was alone.

My thoughts returned to the Church. I visited Monsignor Giblin in Nyack and had a long talk with this cultivated and sophisticated man. I had never regretted the decision that had alienated me from the Church—while Charlie was alive.

The Church had rejected me when I married Charlie, and though I doggedly and defiantly spent the next thirty years of my married life officially outside it, I often attended services—of any denomination, in any language. I hadn't given anything up. I was simply in conflict. I had to choose between the Church and the man God picked out for me. My choice was clear. I was 24, and half expected the heavens to fall on me. This was my only rebellion and a most unlikely change of script. It was my cardinal sin, loving my husband more than anything in this or any other world.

Now he was gone, and I was lost without him. Suddenly, in perspective, those rules and regulations I had once thought so unfair seemed the only law possible. In a sweeping gesture of magnanimity, I absolved the Pope of all guilt and found myself confessing my sins. It was then I found myself in shock.

There was that cold day I walked down Third Avenue. My favorite rosary, out of the drawer, was in my muff. I walked and battled it out with myself. If I returned to the fold, I would have, in effect, to accept that my beautiful life with my husband had been a sin. Could I do it? One thing was certain: without Charlie, I could not go on without going "home."

In my many talks with Monsignor Giblin, I found comfort in his liberal interpretation of my problem. He assured me that my life with Charlie had not been a sin; I had simply broken a Church law.

There were just as many friends who disapproved of my my return to the Church as ever deplored my leaving it. But more and more, I felt the need to give my faith a form once more. I knew Charlie would understand that even sturdy, dependable Helen was the frailest of creatures and needed strength to prevail without him.

I reminded Charlie that it was going to have to take the whole Roman Catholic Church to replace him.

14

THE worst constructed play is a Bach fugue when compared to life. All plays, successful or not, have direction, a point of departure, a pattern—a peculiar logic. A play is considered bad when one or more of its characters acts out of character, illogically. Even in theatre of the absurd, the mood and stage are set. One comes not only to welcome the unexpected, but to expect it as well. Logic is transformed into illogic; black becomes white. But it's all one and the same, really. John is still John, even if he is called Jane.

Whatever the point of view, the accommodating audience, eager to be pleased, soon catches on and is carried along with the fancy. The curtain goes up and eventually comes down. There is a beginning, and—if the Aristotelian middle is no longer there—at least, there is still the end. The actor learns his lines, his entrances and exits. He studies and re-hearses his business and then gets on with it.

But in life there is no such careful planning. Friends who are treasured for their love and loyalty are capable of betrayal. Antagonists whose ill will one considers almost comfortingly constant in this ever-changing world may suddenly act with disarming nobility. One sometimes needs a program.

The good die young—but not always. The wicked prevail —but not consistently. I am confused by life and I feel safe in the confines of the theatre. O'Neill's dramas are slapstick farces, Albee's riddles are simple explanations, Pinter's threatening and threatened anti-heroes are innocent babes— next to life and the living.

I cry out for order and find it only in art. I think, now that I needn't work any longer and still do, it is because the theatre offers form and meaning, and always has. When I do a play, everything is in its place, like my handkerchief drawer, and all's right with the world. I examine my part, learn my lines, and become the character. There are limits to my vices and virtues, boundaries to the good and bad I can do. It's all so tidy and such a relief!

Would that an actor could do his job and then call it a day. But if he has done his job well for a long enough time, the public expects much more of him. If any young actor dreams that stardom is a trip to heaven, while packing his bags, he'd do well to choose his wardrobe with a much hotter climate in mind.

The demands of stardom are relentless. The positive aspects are too numerous and obvious to belabor. As Charlie used to say, it "entitles one to be a first-class passenger with all the special privileges."

But there are times when the duties and responsibilities

outweigh the advantages. Stardom can be a gilded slavery
—and to so many. Not only to the public, but to producers,
investors, press, colleagues, madmen, tuft-hunters—and that
cruelest master of all, one's own standards..

If the would-be star is not born with sympathy for the
weak and vulnerable, he had better develop it fast. The demands upon one's strength are endless and have little to do
with one's work.

Strangers importune you for advice and involvement in
areas better suited to the family doctor or the clergy. To
offer this solicited help is a tremendous responsibility as well
as a burden. To refuse makes one feel cold and remote—
adjectives too easily descriptive of a star.

It is a dilemma and, in my usual way, I have usually grabbed it by its horns. If, indeed, there is a secret to surviving
tragedy, it is not one to keep to yourself. One has to advertise
Acceptance and one should share Faith. And so, rebellious
as I may feel at times, the letters go out, the people are seen,
the speeches are made.

In a sense, later in my career—when I had proved whatever it was that had to be proved and much of the challenge
had gone out it of it—I came to use my station and its attending influence to satisfy other deep needs. I am grateful
that position allows me to embrace many other interests.

Charlie used to laugh at all my activities. "Helen, you're
a do-gooder!" he used to say.

Certainly, I know I need approval, and I couldn't mind
admiration or I wouldn't have been an actress all these years,
but we in the theatre are paradoxes. Our agonizing shyness
is equalled only by the tremendous need for acceptance.
Actors are forever caught in this vise. More than anything,
this admixture might easily be what is considered temperament.

I recall one day waiting in a doorway during a shower.

Two women, fresh from a matinee, stared at me with distressing candor as they whispered to each other.

I shocked myself, as well as them. "Why don't you take a *good* look?" I snapped.

One of the women answered. "If you knew how much we love you, you would forgive us."

I could have cut my tongue out. But I was tired and fretful that day.

I don't always have the diplomacy of an ambassador or the patience of a saint. After all, I'm neither. I am a worker who can tire after a performance, and I am a woman. There are times I want space around me—a moat, if you will, privacy—and I have no right to it.

Unlike any other professional, the actor is expected to be "on" at all times—glamorous, well groomed, in full command of himself, and available. The public expects this of its favorites. The first requisite of a star is a willingness to crush forever the revulsion of living publicly. There ought to be classes in how to meet the responsibilities of stardom.

The public often shares the nervousness of the actor—like the man who recognized me one night on the last bus back to Nyack. It was wartime and there was no gas for the family car.

Up front I watched the man's wife urging him to come back to speak to me and finally he did.

"I want you to know, Miss Hayes, what an inspiration it is to see you riding this bus. My wife wanted me to say to you 'If this bus is good enough for us, it's good enough for Helen Hayes.'"

To which I add, yea, verily.

All theatrical celebrities share a common experience. How often I have heard:

"You look so much like Helen Hayes. Did anyone ever tell you that?"

"You remind me of someone. Now let me see. . . ."

I believe we have all gone through the one that always begins with, "You have no idea how you've altered my life. . . ."

It was in Mykonos that the proprietess of the hotel continued in this vein, ". . . I was pregnant and saw you in *Broken Blossoms* and I sat in the dark praying that the child would be like you and she is and I'm so grateful."

I spent the rest of my stay on the island avoiding this woman, so she'd never discover that I wasn't Lillian Gish.

It is amazing how strongly affected people can be by the theatre and those of us in it. Sometimes fans will break through a mob and get to their favorite, only to burst into tears. Actors have to be nimble to avoid mayhem.

On tour some time ago, I was in a hotel elevator in Ann Arbor, Michigan. The only other passenger was a businessman attending a convention. He evidently felt that as momentary traveling companions we could go on to a lasting friendship. He stared so familiarly that I was forced to nod politely. It was a mistake.

"You have got to meet me and my friends tonight, Miss Hayes," he now suggested. "*We're* different."

Just how different I never discovered. But I can only assume that he hadn't quite articulated what he meant.

A lady in Detroit was more direct. I was working for the National Foundation. As head of the women's division, I visited strategic places around the country. It was during a tour of *Mrs. McThing,* so I was doubling in brass.

One afternoon, the local chapter held a reception for a large group of volunteer workers who were receiving an award. I personally greeted, congratulated and shook hands with all four hundred of them. The line seemed endless when I suddenly looked into the eyes of the dearest old lady.

She had on a dark suit with a lacy jabot and she wore a skimmer with daisies. In her late 70s, she had a tiny, translucent face. I took her white-gloved hand, thanking her for her efforts.

"Oh, my," she exclaimed, "I can take no credit for any of that, dear. I'm only here with a friend. You see, *my* special interest is sex deviation."

* * *

My inability to play the prima donna proved quite a blow during the run of *Victoria.*

I was at the apogee of my career, earning not only adulation but a fortune as well. My successful radio show, *The New Penny,* preceded my Broadway appearances on Tuesday evenings so closely that a police escort got me cross town from N.B.C. to the Broadhurst Theatre on time. In the days of radio, it was possible for me to play any role dressed and made up for Victoria, so that I could walk directly onto the stage when I arrived.

With my MGM contract in effect and my films playing, the newspapers called me "Triple Threat Helen." Those were truly golden days, and I didn't know what to do with all the money I was making.

Each evening I would walk down 44th Street on my way to the theatre. One particular day, I overheard two women who were almost abreast of me.

"There's Helen Hayes," announced the first.

Oh dear, I thought, *I wish to God I could just walk the street in peace.*

"No, it isn't," the other woman said.

"Of course it is. I've certainly seen her often enough on stage."

"I tell you it's impossible. Do you really think that Helen Hayes would be seen in a curled-up nutria coat?"

"I suppose not," the first lady surrendered.

I was appalled. It is true that I have never liked spending a lot of money on clothes. It may just be my background; as I've mentioned, my indifference to style has driven friends crazy. It earned me the reputation at 24 of being dowdy.

One evening, when I arrived at a "do" in a hat and suit that evidently created a chic effect, stylish Kitty Miller happily cried, "At last!"

But that was simply an accident, and everything soon went back to normal.

Nevertheless, those two ladies in the street were my public and they now convinced me that I was cheating them. I quickened my step and called Revillon Frères, the furriers, from my dressing room. I was filled with stylish purpose.

"This is Helen Hayes and I want a sable coat," I announced.

Mr. Tyler had been right. I was going to look the part at last.

"I want one quickly," I added, as if it were a painkiller. Still smarting from my eavesdropping, I had to have those sables immediately.

One of the Frères was at the theatre that afternoon. He arrived in a sable-lined greatcoat with an astrakhan collar. In a portmanteau, he carried sable pelts, which he now laid out on the floor to be examined. I found myself petting the beautiful things.

Darn it, I thought. *There's going to be a change, a new Helen—if not exactly of Troy, at least of Nyack.*

My chic Charlie was going to be proud of his soignée, fur-bearing wife. As for those two ladies, from now on they'd know a real star when they saw one on her way to work.

Monsieur waited while I made up and prepared for the matinee and then he informed "Victoria" of the price of the coat. It was a queen's ransom. I swallowed hard but, still in firm possession of India, gave him the order.

After the matinee that very day, I was taxiing across 57th Street past the Durand Ruell Gallery when I spied a Renoir in the window. Fatefully, the taxi—in traffic—stopped in front of the gallery. I took a long look at Renoir's girl. She looked exactly as I dreamed Mary would when grown up.

"Here's your fare, Driver."

I was out of the cab and in the gallery in three seconds flat. I walked out only after buying the beguiling *Girl in the Lace Hat.*

It was the same price as the sable coat. If the two ladies ever saw me again in the street, they doubtless continued their argument. Because I continued wearing my nutria, doomed forever to Plain Janedom.

Maybe I've endured because of it. I sometimes think that I am the triumph of the familiar over the exotic. Maybe I have proved that to be unfashionable is to survive the changing fashions.

When I did, out of conscientiousness, try to be glamorous, it didn't work anyway. Charlie adored Hattie Carnegie, and I went to her one day and asked if she'd supervise some purchases, which she gladly did. She was wearing a divine suit that afternoon and I so admired it that she made it up for me—but an exact copy. It was about a thousand dollars. With some pretty Delman slippers and a coral rose pin surrounded by diamonds which Gilbert Miller had given to me, I went off to meet the press one day in Boston. I felt at last that I was properly accoutered.

The interview went off very pleasantly and I read it a week later.

"There she sat," I read, "the Queen of the theatre, looking like a *hausfrau* in some costume jewelry and a little brown suit off the rack. . . ."

I had to laugh. I sent the clipping to Hattie, and asked for a reduction in price. Evidently, I am hopeless. The Renoir gave me greater pleasure anyway.

"Well, I let my public down again," I told Charlie the night I canceled the sable.

"You can always wear the Renoir as a sandwich sign on your way to the theatre," Charlie suggested.

There was really no reason why I couldn't have bought both. I can only gather that I didn't care enough about the coat. The Renoir hung in our house in Nyack for years, becoming such an integral part of the general scene that I would go for days without even seeing it. Eventually, after I was widowed and the children gone, I felt as Somerset Maugham did at his own auction when he said, "I am a wanderer and I am owned by things because I love them so."

I, too, auctioned off many possessions, which do tyrannize. One of them was the Renoir. Through the years I have found it wonderful to acquire, but it is also wonderful to divest. It's rather like exhaling.

*　*　*

Collecting friends is a different matter. These I want to keep forever. I have treasured many close friends since my girlhood, but stardom has made friendship difficult as well.

Someone once said that I was as friendly as an Airedale puppy, but celebrity has made me shy of my effect on others. People find it difficult to bridge the distance they feel exists between us, and I am consequently shut out by many men and women I would enjoy knowing better. People have a tendency either to avoid or impress me, out of their own

shyness, exactly as I have done with others. It is a most
irritating impasse.

Playing *Victoria* really put the finishing touches on the
regal aura that surrounds theatrical stardom. Both fellow
actors and public alike seemed to confuse me with the
monarch herself. Fans would rush over to me and, while
waiting for my autograph, actually say, "Victoria was a *great*
Queen," evidently believing that such approval of the lady
was a compliment to me. I only know that, for someone who
loves to relax and laugh with her fellow players, the *Victoria*
tour with its red-carpeted panoply isolated me in much the
same way as the pomp and circumstance that sets royalty
apart.

One night, on tour in the Northwest, I was alone reading
in my drawing room. I was wretched as I heard the rest of
the cast enjoying a singing bee. I sighed in self-pity as I
pondered the irony of majestic solitude.

A special engine had been attached to the train in order
to take us up and over the top of the Rockies. Now that we
were there, the train stopped so that the engine could be
replaced. The sound of laughter wafted through the train
and I looked out the window. There was snow all around
us and the moon, shining on it, made stars everywhere. It
was a staggering vision and I had to share it with everyone.

Undressed, with greased face and curlers, I hastily threw
on a robe and flung open my door. Like a thing possessed, I
rushed through the car.

"Everyone, turn out the lights and look outside! It's a
miracle of beauty!"

But everyone's eyes were riveted to a much more startling
spectacle—me. Especially one of the English girls—little
Charles MacNaughton's mother, the then Bunty Cobb. A
long sigh escaped her. And then slowly—like a somnabulist
she said, "Just one quick click for *Pic* and I'll die happy!"

I marked Bunty for my friend forever. It may be remembered that it was her little boy who encouraged Jamie to the same *lèse majesté*. By saying what she did, Bunty had hurdled all the synthetic obstacles. She'd cut through all the nonsense and reached me. We became close friends.

If you're wise enough not to take yourself too seriously, you must also encourage others not to, either. But the illusions of the theatre are strong and the Bunty Cobbs are rare. It's a pity. I had learned to be an actress; I never learned to be a star.

* * *

I believe I was playing *Coquette* in Boston, with Charlie visiting for the weekend, when Alec Woollcott showed up. He happened to be in town also and took us to the Governor's Mansion to meet Augustus John. Governor Fuller was famous for his collection of Impressionist paintings and had just commissioned John, a great portraitist of his time, to do his.

After my performance, we went off to meet the artist, who was staying on the top floor of the mansion. Alec led our way, warning us not to make any noise, since the governor and his family were apparently asleep.

"If you move quickly," we heard a voice softly call, "you can make it up here without having to see a one of these damned masterpieces."

The three of us landed in the artist's quarters and shared some Scotch from his toothpaste glass. It was typical of Charlie and Company that we had to meet in this insane fashion.

Augustus John was a huge, bearded bear of a man and his talent was so great that I rather hoped, with this visit, that he'd become interested in doing my portrait. Like all painters, he was intrigued by actresses, and I was flattered to notice that he was appraising me with his trained eye.

I was staying at the Ritz and having people in one evening shortly afterwards, so I invited the artist to join us. It was a most pleasant gathering and people were loath to leave—the last two guests being Woollcott and John. They just kept out-staying each other and I was tired. Charlie had gone back to New York—or California or wherever—and Alec, John, and I seemed to be playing *No Exit*. Neither man would budge. They just continued to out-sit each other.

Alec rarely was out-anythinged. But he was exhausted, and staring daggers at John he announced, "I am going to retire. I suggest that everyone do the same."

When John simply said, "Good night, Alec," Woollcott flounced out in a tantrum.

Not two minutes passed before Augustus John started leering at me, like Hugh Griffiths in *Tom Jones;* he was not dissimilar to the actor in appearance. He now lunged at me, so quickly and so violently that I sprang back from the impact. I fell back against a red-lacquered little secretary and slipped, sliding to the ground and through the tunnel of the painter's legs. It was so quick, so deft, so utterly ridiculous that we both began to laugh.

As I landed, the telephone rang. It was Alec.

"Is that awful man out of there, Helen? After all, I've got to look after Charlie's interests."

"Don't worry," I answered, rubbing my bruised thigh. "His interests are taken care of."

And they were; anything else would have been an anticlimax. The whole evening was a sketch—but I never got my portrait.

❖　❖　❖

My failure to rise to the occasion has caused me to avoid

the advances of the high and mighty whenever possible. I was always either too frightened or too frivolous to play the star successfully.

Through Charlie, I met that beguiling leprechaun, Pat Harrington, of New York's Club Eighteen. He was a darling, irreverent creature, and once, when we happened to be in Indianapolis at the same time, he asked if I would like to see a matinee performance of *Gone With the Wind,* which had just opened there. I had missed it in New York, and the idea of relaxing at that great, big, fat movie with Clark and Vivien and Technicolor was just the most delicious thing I could think of.

The night before our movie date, I received a phone call from Booth Tarkington. I was thrilled to hear from him. Of course I would lunch with him the next afternoon; I hadn't seen him in ages.

He looked more like a benign hawk than ever. He was painfully thin and suffering from Parkinson's disease; his hands shook mightily. No longer able to type, he confessed that he was too shy to dictate a love scene. So, he said, he was finished with novels and now was dictating books on art.

A marvelous host and a great talker, the author could still spin a tale, and they poured out after lunch, one more fascinating than the other. The stories were endless, so I kept peeking at my watch, not wanting to miss Pat and the early show of *Gone With the Wind.*

Here I am with Old Pokey, I shockingly thought, *and I'm going to be late for the movie.*

Yes, if I have one regret, it's that I didn't cultivate more the glorious people I knew instead of going off to a movie. My inner conflict was so great that afternoon that Pat and I only made the last third of the film. To this day, I haven't seen the picture in toto.

But I remember one of Booth Tarkington's stories from

that afternoon. He and William Allen White, along with
Irvin Cobb and George Ade, were fierce drinkers. Booth, for
all his *Penrod and Sam,* was a match for Scott Fitzgerald
and, years before, had cut a swath through Paris that was
not soon forgotten. He was found, one dawn, riding tandem
on the golden statue of St. Joan.

Anyway, these four men were strolling home one evening
after a drinking bout and found, leaning against a building,
an old drunk who—in the semi-light—looked exactly like
Edgar Allan Poe. Intrigued, they hoisted the poor creature
to his feet, took him to Tarkington's, and propped him up in
a chair. The man was stiff, stoned, out like a light.

Irvin Cobb addressed the group solemnly.

"We have with us the master—the pride of American letters, the Lama of Literature, Mr. Edgar Allen Poe. What
tribute can we lay at his feet?" Then one by one, vying with
each other, they lay at the feet of this besotted wretch the
tale each considered his finest. The treasures they poured
into that drunk's ears! The half-remembered nightmares he
must have had!

When the wags had spent themselves, they carried their
guest back to the spot where they found him, arranged him
as he was, and wended their separate ways home.

And I broke away, like a child cutting school, to see a
movie!

*   *   *

Years later, as an older, celebrated woman, with a greater
consciousness of my dignity, I still came out second—this
time with a prince of the Church. It's always a variation on
the same theme. I just can't win.

Father William Wassen, a friend of mine in Mexico, established an orphanage near Mexico City. In his unwillingness
to separate siblings, and with his expansive heart, he and his

Little Brothers are always in need of money. At one particular period a few years ago, he was really desperate; when he was in the States, searching for donors, I took him to see Cardinal Cushing in Boston. I was certain that he would recognize Father Wassen's saintliness and would agree to the spreading around of some of the blessed funds.

The cardinal answered the door himself, in a red cassock and a purple rage, as a large woman flung herself past us out of the door. His Eminence was in high dudgeon about something, and not in the mood for the likes of us.

In my zeal I had called a photographer, thinking that after our audience was over I could arrange a beneficial interview for the good father. Utterly out of character, I was being a public relations man. Cardinal Cushing saw the photographer waiting in the vestibule and became livid. After some hasty explanations, he deferred to our long friendship and brusquely asked us into his study. I introduced the cardinal to Father Wassen, who outlined his work simply and eloquently. I was so proud of him.

His Scowling Eminence was scornful. "You can't do this kind of thing alone. This kind of work should be in the hands of the Dominicans. This is absurd for one man. . . ."

I interrupted to speak of the wonders of the Little Brothers and was immediately put in my place. I was trying to be a buffer between priest and cardinal, and I was definitely off-limits.

After a tirade that seemed endless, Cardinal Cushing unexpectedly ended it.

"I will give you $10,000 of my private funds."

Young Father Wassen's smile was beautiful to behold and I thought of all the Chicos and Pepes who could now fill their bellies. My delight was like a geyser. It had been tough but Helen, thinking positively and conquering with God's will, had done it again. I turned to effuse over the Cardinal, but he continued.

"Yes! I'll make it $10,000 if *anyone* wishes to match it."

The cardinal now glowered at me, his testiness departing as my confusion grew. I had always been, I thought, quite sympathetic and cooperative with the saintly father—but 10,000 was a figure that momentarily paralyzed me.

We were a tableau, we three: Father Wassen basking in the cardinal's gruff charity; I, with God's will, being forced to share it; and His Eminence ready to bring the wrath of God down on me if I didn't. He was after me that day, all right, and though I squared my chin and looked as dignified and inscrutable as I could, by the time we left I had matched the cardinal in only one way.

15

Now that I have reached a goodly age—a grandmother's age, three things remain. Faith, love and
memory.

I don't know how I could go on without faith. How terrible to believe that there is nothing left when the sets are
struck and the show moves on. Nothing but bits of the three-
sheets, fragments of colored posters on peeling walls, covered with the impertinent grafitti of a new generation of
players.

The horror of believing that we strut and fret our hour
on the stage all sound and fury, signifying nothing—and
then never even get to read our reviews.

I can't believe it. I have been in too many plays, acted too
many women, worked too many years not to have got an
inkling of the whole from the pieces, the sum from the parts.
There is the play—but first there is the playwright.

Sensible of this, total faith, I must confess, eludes me. I

have doubted and I will doubt again. I am too questioning not to doubt, not to seek alternatives, other answers, other paths. Still, I eventually return and for this I am grateful.

I stand in envy of those who can believe in intangibles. I pray and I try. I try too hard sometimes but mostly my faith remains solely in what I can see and touch, although these too, alas, fade from view and slip through one's fingers. And so, I behave as well as I am able here in this world in order to assure my place in the next one. My heaven is reunion with those I have loved. If the positive eludes me, so, indeed, does the negative. My mind remains open and, some day perhaps, complete faith will come.

Yes, I have doubted. I have wandered off the path. I have been lost. But I always return. It is beyond the logic I seek. It is intuitive—an intrinsic, built-in sense of direction. I seem always to find my way home. My faith has wavered but has saved me.

As for love, I was exposed to a generous helping of it from the beginning. From Graddy Hayes, from Father, from Aunt Mamie and especially my mother. Mother's great capacity for love outweighed everything else. Led by her, my family fortified me with their love. They taught me how to be confident in loving for it is a most audacious act—to love mortal things. They leave you. They perish. But one must love again. One must adventure endlessly in loving, never fearing pain and loss.

It must have been Graddy, Aunt Mamie and Annie Hess who set the example for the MacArthur household, always crowded with family and friends and pets, filled with objects the children could give their hearts to. Both my children became experts in the art of loving. My house, at this very moment, resounds with the love that has passed through it.

If faith and love have been ephemeral, memory, at least, is constant.

Happily my memory is defective and I remember best the good things, the gay and joyous things, and the most joyous are always those that have to do with Charlie and the world he presented me with.

I remember going to Europe with Charlie in the late '20s. We stayed at Marie and Averell Harriman's on the Avenue Foch. They lent us the apartment for our stay and it was all terribly posh—with Van Goghs and Picassos on the walls and a staff of five in the servants' quarters. Mr. Tyler would have been pleased. I was, at last, living like a star.

But it was when we left the chic apartment that Charlie introduced me to Wonderland. He took me to Gertrude Stein's. If Neysa McMein's or Alec's soirées had floored me, one can only imagine my bewilderment in such an assembly. Dazzled by the collection of paintings and geniuses, nothing impressed me more than Alice B. Toklas's mustache.

They were all there—Pound and Joyce and Hemingway and Sylvia Beach and Scott and Zelda and Duchamp and Man Ray. I was never more surely Mr. Carroll's Alice at the Tea-Party, as I sat listening to the jabberwocky.

Charlie was right at home, and I was welcome because I was his girl. I sometimes marvel at the private feast he set before me. The memories!

I remember Charlie Chaplin—and what a beauty he was —telling us one night his own wonderful stories of the price of fame. He was a great storyteller. Once, in a Paris street, duty called and he entered one of the appropriate kiosks— only to be recognized by the man standing next to him. Eager to share his good fortune, the Parisian ran out into the street, pointing and yelling, "Charlot! Charlot!" and the comedian—not ready to depart—had to stand there, his famous feet and head in full view as all Paris screamed, "Bravo!"

It was at Irving Berlin's apartment one night, before he married Ellin, that Chaplin entertained us with a most unforgettable soliloquy from *Hamlet*. He recited it as the Dane would, had he had catarrh as well as melancholy. It was Hamlet with a nasty nose cold which was "not out of the question in *such* a climate." It was the rest of us who gasped for breath.

I remember listening to the bewitching Noel Coward and Gertrude Lawrence, their tiny bottoms sharing one piano stool, as they sang—not the songs they made famous—but the little cockney ditties they did in London when they were kids, before life had become all plum pudding.

I remember the gentle Harlequin, Harpo Marx, ecstatically practicing on a mute harp, his astonished eyes and hanging tongue never for a second suggesting his musical dedication.

Then there was the treat of seeing Bea Lillie just walk across the room. Or Dotty Parker asking, when Tallulah had made a characteristically profane exit from one, "Has Whistler's Mother gone yet?"

Those dazzlers! Marlene Dietrich, the glorious *Frau*, years ago at Paramount bringing me, each day, some of the hot lunch she insisted on making for her small daughter Maria before she left for the studio. Marlene again, calling on the day that Dr. Jonas Salk made his breakthrough and the polio vaccine became a reality. She just called—with that sensitivity of hers—knowing how much it meant to me.

John Barrymore, as he lay reading *Leaves of Grass* aloud, in front of our fire in Nyack. Lynn Fontanne making me a blonde again in her eternal and fruitless quest to transform me into a glamor girl.

Jascha Heifetz playing the Brahms Violin Concerto just for me at my hotel, after he caught me in a white lie about attending his matinee recital.

Clark Gable, the MGM lion, sending me a mash note through his trusted Oriental manservant, when we worked together a thousand years ago. I'm proud of that. And even

prouder that I ignored it. Years later, when he came backstage to say hello, Clark smiled that dimpled smile—Rhett's
smile. He was married to the shining Carole Lombard then.

"You were too shy, weren't you, Helen?"

Men are marvelous. I learned all about them from knowing only one—but oh, so well. Charlie! I could no more re-
marry than have been unfaithful.

* * *

When I met my grandchildren—first Charlie in New York
and then Mary Hayes in Los Angeles—it was in the first
moment of their lives. Their eyes were blinking, their faces
were scarlet with rage. Both of them seemed like castaways
and I was shocked. Surely, at birth man is the most helpless
of species.

They seemed so abandoned, all alone in the arena—little
Christians thrown to the lions. Joyce, like all new mothers,
was dozing; and Jim and I might just as well have been, for
all the help we could offer.

We simply stared at the classic spectacle with thumbs
turned heavenward. We needn't have worried. Each child
survived, like Androcles collecting on an ancient debt.

I sometimes think that we are a race of Androcleses—all
of us reaping dividends, cutting coupons, beneficiaries of
some providential policy.

Since the beginning of man's recorded story, there has
been a recognition of good and evil and a celebration of
God, no matter His name or semblance. All through the ages,
men have been pointing the way to oases, building resting
places, making it easier for me. To reject their gift is like
spitting on a present.

Despite my days of doubt and my many years outside the
Church—years of worldly pride and impatience with the
dogma that would have robbed me of my own true love—I

never stopped believing. Even Charlie, for all his irreverence and reaction to parental sanctimony, knew in his heart of hearts that we are all touched by the Divine.

One night, Edwin Powell Hubbell, who had been working on a powerful new telescopic lens that would pierce the nebulae, invited Aldous Huxley and Anita Loos with Charlie and me to Mount Wilson Observatory in Pasadena.

We were intrigued by the fact that that tiny bit of glass, which could fit into the socket of one man's eye, could swell out to embrace the whole universe. It seemed to put us in hailing distance of all eternity.

Aldous insisted that, in not too long a time, lenses would become so strong that man would sit in front of the telescope and cut through the atmosphere, the ionosphere, the galaxies themselves, and light upon his own backside. We all laughed, except for fun-loving Charlie. He was suddenly the serious one.

"No, no. That's not at all what's going to happen," he said softly. "We're all getting so big for our britches that we're going to see God's reproachful finger wagging at us—telling us not to be so fresh, reminding us to mind our manners."

I leave you with this grandmotherly advice.